Enforcing community sentences: supervisors' perspectives on ensuring compliance and dealing with breach

by
Tom Ellis
Carol Hedderman
Ed Mortimer

A Research and Statistics Directorate Report

Home Office
Research and
Statistics
Directorate

London: Home Office

Home Office Research Studies

The Home Office Research Studies are reports on research undertaken by or on behalf of the Home Office. They cover the range of subjects for which the Home Secretary has responsibility. Titles in the series are listed at the back of this report (copies are available from the address on the back cover). Other publications produced by the Research and Statistics Directorate include Research Findings, the Research Bulletin, Statistical Bulletins and Statistical Papers.

The Research and Statistics Directorate

The Directorate consists of three Units which deal with research and statistics on Crime and Criminal Justice, Offenders and Corrections, Immigration and General Matters; the Programme Development Unit; the Economics Unit; and the Operational Research Unit.

 The Research and Statistics Directorate is an integral part of the Home Office, serving the Ministers and the department itself, its services, Parliament and the public through research, development and statistics. Information and knowledge from these sources informs policy development and the management of programmes; their dissemination improves wider public understanding of matters of Home Office concern.

First published 1996

Application for reproduction should be made to the Information and Publications Group, Room 1308, Home Office, Apollo House, 36 Wellesley Road, Croydon CR9 3RR.

Foreword

If sentencers and the wider public are to have confidence in community sentences, the terms of such orders must be clear, they must be directed towards addressing offending, they must be complied with, and the response to non- compliance must be quick and appropriate.

This study was commissioned to discover how probation and community service staff ensure that offenders comply with the terms of a probation or community service order, when they decide to breach an offender, and how the breach process functions.

The results suggest that, despite the introduction of National Standards for the Probation Service, enforcement practices varied not only between areas but between teams and officers. This lack of system has resulted in pockets of poor practice, but it has also facilitated some enterprising and innovative approaches to encouraging compliance and dealing with breach.

CHRIS LEWIS
Head of Offenders and Corrections Unit
Research and Statistics Directorate
September 1996

Acknowledgements

The authors would like to thank all of the members of the probation services, magistrates' courts and police forces who granted us access, agreed to be interviewed and provided us with information. As we do not name the areas in the report, they will have to remain anonymous here. We would also like to thank Mary Fielder (of the Inspectorate of Probation), Julie Vennard, John Maggi and Margaret Ayres from the Research and Statistics Directorate and George Mair (John Moores University) for their contributions. Finally, thanks are due to Professor Ken Pease (University of Huddderfield) for providing the independent peer review.

Tom Ellis
Carol Hedderman
Ed Mortimer

Contents

Summary

Sentencers have increasingly been encouraged to use community sentences as ways of punishing and deterring offenders as well as assisting in their rehabilitation. Indeed the combination order, introduced in the Criminal Justice Act 1991, is an explicit expression of this approach, combining service in the community with probation supervision, while being more demanding than either form of sentence in isolation. But legislation alone is clearly not enough. If community sentences are to be seen as a hard rather than a soft option, the terms of such orders must be clear, they must be directed towards addressing offending behaviour, they must be complied with, and the response to non-compliance must be quick and appropriate.

This study was commissioned to examine the methods used by probation and community service (CS) staff to ensure compliance, the circumstances in which they decide to breach an offender, and how the breach process functions. Interviews were carried out between September 1994 and December 1995 in five probation areas with a total of 89 probation and CS staff, 19 magistrates and 31 police officers. Each area was also asked to provide copies of local enforcement guidelines. Although interviews took place in two areas after the introduction of revised National Standards (NS) in March 1995, all five services were still operating under the 1992 Standards.

Similarities and differences between areas

The results of this study suggest that, despite the introduction of the 1992 National Standards for the Probation Service, covering the full range of their work, enforcement practices differed within and between areas.

Local guidelines

Only one of the five areas visited had produced a comprehensive enforcement policy document.

Guidelines for preparing and prosecuting breach cases were covered in staff handbooks and manuals in all five areas, but procedures for dealing with failures to comply on probation orders tended to be covered in ad hoc memos, issued as problems arose.

Local CS guidelines were more systematised than those for probation, probably because CS requirements are intrinsically simpler than probation. This may explain why CS staff also showed a greater willingness to work to such guidelines, but the fact that they tend to have different backgrounds to probation officers may also have been influential.

Non-compliance and breach

In all five areas, repeated failure to attend without a reasonable explanation was the most common reason for non-compliance and, consequently, for initiating breach proceedings. Breaches for other reasons were more likely on CS orders and, to a lesser extent, on probation orders with requirements. Probation and CS officers also noted that failures to attend were easier to prove in court than other types of non-compliance.

Probation and CS officers said they recommended that magistrates allowed an order to continue (with a warning about future conduct and/or a small fine) when using breach proceedings to ensure compliance. They recommended revocation and re-sentencing where an order had broken down or where the offender had made no effort to start the order.

The police were criticised by probation respondents for being slow to enforce warrants when an offender failed to answer a summons.

The speed at which breaches came to court varied from three weeks to two months. Probation officers complained that as a result of court delays some cases took so long that the order had been completed and no further action could be taken against the offender.

Combination orders

The enforcement of combination orders was considered problematic by most of the probation officers and CS staff interviewed because they were sometimes imposed by courts on offenders who were incapable of meeting the additional demands they imposed. There was also poor communication between CS and probation supervisors.

Monitoring systems

The contrast between CS and probation order monitoring systems was very noticeable in all areas. CS systems were up-to-date and computerised. For probation orders, senior probation officers (SPOs) relied on both retrospective manual casefile sampling and probation officers alerting them to enforcement problems. Since SPOs effectively relied on supervising officers to record all failures to comply and/or bring them to their attention, it is doubtful whether these methods would uncover all unsatisfactory enforcement practice.

At least one area is developing its own comprehensive systems and others may follow. Clearly, it is important that developments in local systems and the national 'Case Records Administration and Management system' (CRAMS) are linked.

Training

Existing training focused on the breach process and preparing for and presenting cases at court. No specific training was available on ensuring compliance.

None of the 36 CS officers or sessional workers interviewed had received any formal training in either CS work in general, or in the enforcement process specifically.

National Standards and enforcement practice

It is clear that most probation and CS officers thought that the 1992 National Standards were helpful in ensuring fair and consistent enforcement practice, and allowed them to use discretion where necessary.

It was also clear that probation officers did not employ the Standards strictly – for example, recording an attendance when the offender turned up the same week rather than at the time and day they had specified.

Some probation officers indicated that they might ignore any attempt to reduce their discretion in ways which they considered would interfere with productive work with offenders.

While magistrates generally applauded the introduction of National Standards (crediting them with enhancing the quality of breach case presentations), they saw no need to be familiar with the contents of the Standards or even to act in accordance with them – as they were for the Probation Service, not the courts.

Lessons for practice

Most SPOs encouraged probation officers to revoke orders early for good progress. SPOs thought that this was an incentive to offenders to comply with an order, but it was also used to reduce high caseloads. However, in the long run, this could have a negative effect if the quality of the progress made by the offender may become a secondary consideration to the desire to reduce officer workload.

Probation officers in two areas used 'low grade reporting', for offenders who were 'troublesome' or 'unco-operative'. In other words, offenders reported to a probation office or probation day centre, but supervisors had little active contact with them. While some may see this as a way of freeing up time to work with better motivated offenders, it may also be construed as an inappropriate response which could put the public at risk.

Some probation officers dealt with missed appointments by putting the offender on a more frequent reporting cycle. This may be useful in cases where the non-compliance is wilful but other probation officers thought that for offenders with chaotic lifestyles this practice might increase the chances of failing their order.

The research showed that individual probation officers had made use of a variety of techniques for ensuring that offenders attended their appointments. These included the use of appointment cards, co-ordinating appointments with signing-on days for unemployed offenders, or keeping offenders on fortnightly reporting at the same time and day of the week for the duration of an order.

In one area, on a first failure to attend, probation officers could refer offenders for a visit by a 'follow up' officer who tried to trace offenders who had moved address without having notified the probation service. Although no hard evidence was available, probation officers and the follow up officer considered this to be a more effective way of ensuring compliance than sending warning letters by post.

Special breach courts were held in four of the five areas in this study. They were set up so that cases could be listed to a particular day, rather than arranging each hearing separately. This ensured that probation officers could take this into account in arranging their workloads.

1 Introduction

Since the late 1980s, the Government has actively sought to change the position of community penalties in relation to other sentences through the publication of Green and White Papers, and through the publication and revision of National Standards covering supervision and enforcement of orders. Sentencers and the public were encouraged in the 1988 Green Paper Punishment, Custody and the Community (Home Office, 1988) to view Community Sentence Orders and Probation Supervision as ways of punishing, as well as deterring, incapacitating offenders and assisting in their rehabilitation. This shift of emphasis resulted in the introduction of the Combination Order under the Criminal Justice Act 1991, which combines community service with probation supervision and is intended to be more demanding and restrictive of liberty than either as an individual sentence. These moves may, in part, explain why sentencers have made increasing use of community disposals for serious offences throughout this period: so that of the 313,400 offenders sentenced for indictable offences in 1994, 24 per cent received probation, community service or combination orders, compared to only 18 per cent in 1990[1] (Home Office, 1995b: 158).

Clearly, if this upward trend is to continue, and if the Probation Service is to respond to the challenge of supervising offenders convicted of serious offences the terms of community sentence orders must be clear, they must be directed towards addressing offending behaviour, they must be complied with, and the response to non-compliance must be quick and appropriate.

Aims of the study

The aims of this study are to examine practitioners' perspectives on the enforcement process. It considers how they ensure compliance, how they arrive at the decision to breach, and how, once breach action is taken, the enforcement process functions. The study covers probation, community service (CS) and combination orders, and focuses particularly on the following areas:

---

1   Combination orders were not available in 1990. They accounted for 2.6 per cent of indictable offence disposals in 1994.

- the formal enforcement process, including the role of National Standards and perceptions of them

- the identification of practical enforcement methods, and variations in these practices within and between different probation services, as well as across different types of community order

- the identification of common obstacles to successful enforcement

- the identification of good practice in the enforcement process.

Research methods

The first stage of this research involved examining recent research material on community penalties, and other non-custodial penalties with comparable enforcement practices, in England and Wales. This review showed that despite the vast research literature on community penalties, very little of it concentrated on enforcement and breach practices.

Those studies which covered enforcement issues were examined to draw out common themes and practices. A semi-structured questionnaire was constructed for probation staff, magistrates and police officers, based on this material, but allowing space for new topics or angles to emerge in discussion.

The study took place in five probation areas where the authors aimed to interview about 15 to 20 probation and CS staff, four magistrates and four police officers per area. In practice, 89 probation and CS staff were interviewed about, the effect of the 1992 NS, local enforcement guidelines, ensuring compliance and the use of discretion, breach procedures, and court action. All interviewees were guaranteed confidentiality, and the areas were also anonymised to further safeguard the identity of individual respondents.

Nineteen magistrates were interviewed about breach courts, probation and probation liaison committees, PSR proposals, breach report recommendations, and the effect of NS. Thirty-one police officers (or civilian equivalent) were interviewed regarding the prioritisation, monitoring and execution of community penalty warrants, and about their attitude to community orders in general. As far as possible, we attempted to cover a number of offices in different settings within each probation service, and to incorporate the full range of personnel involved, from ACPOs to CS sessional workers (see Annex I).

Interviews were carried out between September 1994 and December 1995. In considering the results described in this report, it is important to bear in mind that the National Standards published in 1992 were in force in all areas during this time. The current revised Standards were published in March 1995, but while interviews were carried out in two of the five areas after this date, neither of them had yet implemented the new Standards (see Annex II).

The areas in the study were chosen using data from the Probation Index as a rough guide to different patterns of breach (whether breach led to continuation or revocation), and to ensure a mix of metropolitan, shire and other urban areas. As there were some reservations about the completeness of the data, the figures have not been reproduced here.

Each area was asked to provide copies of local enforcement guidelines which were in force during fieldwork. These were often supplemented by a number of internal memoranda as new enforcement issues arose.

The structure of the report

The next chapter presents a review of the literature on the enforcement of community penalties and non-custodial sentences. Chapter Three outlines the supervision of probation and CS orders and the formal enforcement systems in place in the study areas; and Chapter Four looks at practical methods employed to ensure compliance, as well as issues and problems arising from these. Chapter Five covers issues arising from the breach process, both prior to and at court (including interviews with magistrates and police). Overall conclusions and lessons for practice are outlined in Chapter Six.

2 A review of previous research on enforcement

Introduction

This review summarises the main findings from studies which examined, among other things, enforcement of community penalties in England and Wales. In carrying out the review, it quickly became obvious that enforcement and/or breach practices have rarely been the main focus of research studies on community orders.[1] The review concentrates mainly on probation orders, CS orders and combination orders, since these are the focus of our research, but also considers some literature on attendance centres, probation and bail hostels, money payment supervision orders, and fines and compensation orders. The chapter ends with a summary of the key enforcement issues identified from the available literature.

Probation orders

The research literature indicates contrasting attitudes of probation officers toward the dual roles of care and control when supervising an order. For instance, Lawson (1978) found evidence that lack of experience, idealism and unfamiliarity with court procedure sometimes inhibited probation officers from taking breach action. On the other hand, Sheppard (1980) found that most probation officers saw no need to separate control and treatment functions, and were happy to rely on their professional judgement in deciding whether to instigate breach proceedings (see also Giller and Morris, 1978; and Davies, 1979). However, most studies agree that probation officers gave a relatively low priority to enforcement. Indeed, in one of the few studies which specifically focused on the enforcement of probation orders (prior to CJA 1991 and the introduction of the 1992 National Standards) Andrew Willis (1981) argued that both offenders and probation officers were concerned less with control than with employment, financial and domestic issues (see also Lawson, 1978; Sheppard, 1980; and Broad, 1991). Willis also noted the routine use of discretion in the enforcement process. Over a decade later, Humphrey and Pease (1992: 42) still found evidence of this approach. One supervising officer in their study noted – *"If*

---

1   There are a number of recent procedural guides to breach process (eg, see Moore and Wilkinson, 1994: 119-127; Stone, 1994 and Ward and Ward, 1993: 85-104), which have not been covered here.

they manage to fall in here once a month and you can get them in a car and take them to the community drugs team and that happens once every six weeks, then that probably does more good than failing three weeks on the trot and you taking them back to court and breaching them".

In contrast, Drakeford (1993: 293) argued that since the 1991 Criminal Justice Act, individual probation officers felt pressurised to believe that *"a good probation officer is a breaching probation officer, and likely to be evaluated on that basis".* Broad (1991: 99) also warned NS might result in automatic breaching of offenders after a minimum number of failures to attend, without adequate investigation of the reasons for non-attendance. However, the 1992-93 HM Inspectorate of Probation (HMIP) Annual Report (1993: 35) noted that there was still *"extraordinary variation"* in the management of probation orders, and some staff were found to be uncertain about the use of their professional discretion within the framework of the NS.[2] HMIP looked to probation managers to help probation officers use their authority and discretion *"in appropriate and accountable ways"* (HMIP Annual Report 1993:40), but successive Quality and Effectiveness (Q&E) inspections[3] have revealed that there is still variation between probation areas in the point at which breach is taken. In addition, recent thematic inspections of community service (HM Inspectorate of Probation, 1995a), dealing with dangerous people (HM Inspectorate of Probation, 1995b) and probation orders with additional requirements (HM Inspectorate of Probation, 1996a) criticised uneven and unsatisfactory enforcement practices throughout the Probation Service.

In an attempt to balance professional discretion with the new demands of the NS, Drakeford (1993: 299-300) recommended a 'minimalist approach' to enforcement. He emphasised the discretion contained in the Standards, especially for offenders with chaotic or impulsive lifestyles, and thought that local practices should reflect this in addition to their concentration on failures to comply.

Drakeford went on to argue that a test of 'normality', according to offenders' circumstances, should be applied in deciding whether to take breach action, and that the original sentencer, or a Senior Probation Officer, should explore the possibility of taking no action to the fullest extent. He also suggested no breach action should be taken for three missed appointments, unless one offer of a home visit has been made and deliberately declined (see also Vass, 1990:122-3, for CS practices). Lastly, in order to ensure consistency and quality of service across teams, Drakeford put forward the idea of breach gatekeeping panels to oversee problematic cases. He concluded that this

---

2   The most recent annual report found that "enforcement of probation orders was being tackled more energetically than previously" (HM Inspectorate of Probation, 1995a: 26).
3   HMIP examines the implementation of NS in the supervision of community orders in all its Q&E inspections.

approach might lessen the risk of further punishment for less serious offenders due to probation officers' *"lazy adherence"* to rigid requirements (1993: 301).

McWilliams and Pease (1990) argued for the opposite approach to Drakeford: that statutory control had always been part of the probation officer's role, and should be faced squarely: *"Probation officers who collude with the evasion of court-mandated control give the opposite communication to that required"* (1990: 22). McWilliams and Pease saw the proliferation of local 'codes of practice' as an attempt to limit the powerful element of discretion. In direct contrast to Drakeford, they stated that one of the major problems created by codes of practice was the resultant 'minimum professional practice' at the expense of 'good professional practice' (ibid). Perhaps more importantly for our study, McWilliams and Pease argued that codes of practice were likely to force probation officers into more covert types of discretion (this is also discussed in relation to CS orders and ancillary staff below). Indeed, Humphrey and Pease (1992: 39) in a later study, found probation officers claimed that their seniors would only be aware of problems if they brought them to their attention. This indicates that casefile checks by SPOs may be of dubious value as a method of uncovering poor enforcement practice by supervising officers.

Community Service orders

Historically, probation orders have been given to offenders in need of structured social work help, while the Wootton Report (1970)[4] established CS, from the outset as a disposal for constructive punishment, comprising of a blend of punishment, reparation and rehabilitation. Perhaps as a result of these different aims, most of the literature on enforcement practice for community sentences concentrates on CS.

Despite the difference in emphasis between probation and CS orders, Young (1979), ten years before the introduction of NS for CS, found that CS supervisors tended to concentrate on the social and personal problems of an individual, rather than on their attendance records. Perhaps as a result, the number of CS disposals began to decline by 1985, and the Home Office was concerned that sentencers were losing confidence in the disposal (Lloyd, 1991). However, since the introduction of National Standards in April 1989, Lloyd noted that the decline had been reversed and the number of orders terminated for breach had increased.[5]

---

4   The ideas embodied in the Wootton Report, officially known as the report published by the Advisory Council on the Penal System – 'Non-custodial and Semi-custodial Penalties' (1970), London: HMSO – were incorporated into the CJA 1972. CS schemes were set up in six pilot areas following the new legislation, and by 1979, all probation services had introduced them.

5   CS disposals continued to rise, reaching 49,500 in 1994. The proportion of offenders breaching CS orders rose to a high of 30 per cent in 1990, but has since continued to decline to 24 per cent in 1994 (Home Office, 1995b: 170; 182).

Differences between areas

Pease et al. (1975) and Pease and West (1977) found that offenders serving CS orders were generally evaluated on failures to attend, rather than on their performance when attending. They argued that, since CS in different probation services had varying levels of flexibility for recording lateness and absences, this was unfair.[6] Other studies have also found variations in practice (see for instance: Young, 1979; McWilliams and Murphy, 1980; Read, 1980; Pease, 1985; Vass, 1986).

Skinns (1990: 69) in a piece of research carried out just prior to the introduction of NS found two quite different approaches to enforcing CS orders. In 'Northern City' probation officers were responsible for breach decisions. Breach action was initiated routinely for absences, but a high level of 'troublesomeness' was tolerated and rarely led to breach action. Further, breach did not always lead to the offender being taken to court. Instead, cases were reviewed, with only 40 per cent being taken to court, often as a 'disciplinary device'. These offenders were usually fined and allowed to continue the order (ibid.).

In 'Eastern County', formal rules were enforced by paid sessional workers on group placements, although on individual placements, offenders were supervised by volunteers who did not always apply enforcement rules as readily as paid staff. Again, breaches were mainly instigated for absences, rather than unsatisfactory work or behaviour (ibid.: 73). However, in contrast to 'Northern City', breach action tended to be restricted to a smaller number of cases which were certain to result in termination, and were characterised by a long and difficult pre-breach period.

Skinns' (1990) study confirms Pease and West's (1977) concern that CS orders were enforced unevenly in different probation areas. At the time of Skinns' research, the impending NS were already being used to structure practice in all probation areas (ibid.: 78). However, 'Northern City' had developed a breach approach that needed little change (ibid.: 75), whereas in 'Eastern County', practices would have to be revised to a much greater extent (see also Wilkinson, 1990).

Organisation of CS supervision and enforcement

In Vass's study, published in 1989, but based on data from the late 1970s, CS orders were supervised under the authority of probation officers, although

---

6   Harris and Webb (1983) found in their study of supervision orders, that missing an appointment was the most common failure to comply after re-offending (since the CJA 1991 orders do not have to be breached for re-offending). It was also unusual for supervisors to punish offenders for failures to comply.

these officers generally disliked CS, because it concentrated on practical tasks and not real 'social work'.

Vass found that probation officers made special concessions to offenders, in return for their co-operation. This in turn resulted in *"a regular and consistent output of offenders completing their CSOs despite consistent violations of the terms of their orders"*, but giving the impression that CS was very successful and well run (Vass, 1989: 260).

Vass (1989) also found that the day-to-day supervision of CS work projects fell mainly on the low status, poorly paid ancillary workers without professional qualifications. These ancillary staff felt marginalised by their supervising probation officers, and suffered from low job satisfaction and status. As a result, they often resorted to informal practices to reduce conflicts with offenders, which ran counter to strict enforcement methods e.g., recording an inflated number of hours worked by the offenders; not punishing poor standards of work (Vass 1989: 261).

Vass (1990: 130) equated these informal enforcement practices with police cautioning: expanding the opportunities for offenders to remain in the community instead of custody. He argued that attempts within the criminal justice system to make enforcement practice more rigid and coercive by eliminating overt opportunities for discretion, might only make those practices less visible and perhaps less desirable (ibid.: 167-168). These informal practices are defined by Vass (1990:120) as an unstated 'code of conduct'. As long as an offender contacted a supervisor with a satisfactory explanation of absence, breach could be avoided.

Vass also argued that the use of discretion established a dialogue of trust and a common aim between offender and supervisor and the successful completion of the order (ibid.: 121). Formal enforcement methods would only be employed if that relationship broke down. Indeed, Vass argued that breach action was usually initiated because offenders had violated the informal 'code of conduct', rather than formal breach requirements (1990: 126).

Vass found that some offenders 'worked' the informal system, so that their absenteeism appeared irregular, thus preventing coercive supervisor action. Vass also described the use of disciplinary interviews and he regarded these as part of a formal enforcement process (Vass, 1990: 124-5). However, where offenders were unco-operative and unrepentant, supervisors still tried to find explanations which avoided immediate breach. Considerations of time and expense also led to some delay or avoidance in initiating breach proceedings (1990: 127-128).

Following the introduction of NS for CS in 1989, Lloyd (1991) found that most of those failing to attend CS orders were breached after three absences, and that there had been a decline in those breached for four or more absences, suggesting that NS had been heeded. Lloyd concluded that rigorous breach policy, even if it led to greater use of custody, increased the confidence of sentencers in CS disposals. However, he warned that the potential rise in the number of offenders receiving custodial sentences, on revocation of their CS orders, might offset any increase in the use of the order for more serious offenders. Secondly, sentencers might become irritated, in the long run, with the number of 'trivial' breaches brought before them, and make less CS disposals (Lloyd, 1991).

Combination orders

Combination orders were introduced under CJA 1991, and were originally intended as a disposal for more serious offences at the Crown Court, but in practice, magistrates have made more frequent use of them.[7]

Magistrates also imposed more combination orders than were proposed in PSRs (see Home Office, 1993; Francis, 1993; Heritage, 1993; Mair et al. 1994; and Moloney, 1995), especially for offenders who had committed more serious offences. Unfortunately, these offenders are often least likely to meet the demands of a combination order due to their chaotic lifestyles or antipathy toward authority (Home Office, 1993: 39).

The dual nature of combination orders also led to those serving straight CS orders and those completing the CS component of a combination order being treated differently when it came to enforcement. Moloney (1995: 27-28) and Mair et al. (1994: 18, 32, 34, 35, 39, 41, 42) found that CS officers tended to regard probation officers as too lenient when judging explanations of absences, and probation officers thought that CS officers were often too inflexible in their approach to breach. The level of liaison between probation and CS officers was also problematic: CS officers thought they got the 'worst deal' (Moloney, 1995: 25), in that probation officers were less likely to share information with them than vice versa (see also Mair et al., 1994: 26, 33, 35).

Attendance centres

Mair (1991) found that the most successful Senior Attendance Centres

---

7   For all offenders in 1994, 9,898 combination order disposals were made at magistrates' courts, compared to 2,730 at the Crown Court (Home Office, 1996). The respective figures for PSR proposals were 4,982 and 5,753 (figures supplied by HO Statistical Division, September 1996).

managed to blend the disciplinary and informal sides of their work (Mair 1991: 166).[8] Although attendance centres were not included in the 1992 NS, enforcement rules were generally in line with them. However, a good deal of discretion and informal enforcement was employed by supervisors at both senior attendance centres (Mair, 1991: 163-164), and in junior attendance centres, where minor infringements could be dealt with by imposing a range of increasingly arduous tasks (Gelsthorpe and Morris, 1983: 109). Consequently, formal enforcement action mostly resulted from failures to attend, as opposed to troublesome behaviour while attending the centres. Mair (1991: 164) also found that absenteeism was dealt with on an individual basis. Offenders who were liked by the supervisors, and who appeared to respond well, were often allowed more absences than were formally acceptable. Gelsthorpe and Morris' findings for junior attendance centres were similar (1983: 109).[9]

Mair (1991: 163) found that enforcement practice also varied according to the levels of local police co-operation. Ideally the police were telephoned as soon as an offender was absent, so that they could visit his or her home. In practice, the level of police enthusiasm varied. Some areas did not attempt to follow up absences immediately and warning letters were sent for a first absence, followed up by a home visit.

Supervisors also mentioned disincentives to take breach action, including: the amount of paperwork required; the need to make a court appearance; the unpopularity of breaches with magistrates; and the feeling that taking an offender back to court was a professional failure.

Probation and bail hostels

Lewis and Mair (1988: 13) found varying enforcement practices in their study of probation and bail hostels. Some hostels issued verbal and written warnings before action on broken rules, while others defined the situation as an emergency in order to evict residents immediately (see also Sinclair, 1971). Simon and Wilson (1975: 38-39) found that the resident staff in bail hostels preferred to handle breach of hostel rules (i.e., bail conditions) themselves, whereas probation officers felt obliged to inform the court of unexplained absences. There was also variation in the way hostel staff classified breaches. If a resident failed to return one night, but returned two days later, some wardens classified this as absconding and returned the offender to court, while others reprimanded the offender but allowed them to remain (see also Lewis and Mair, 1988: 12-13).

---

8   This finding is consistent with Sinclair's (1971) 'firm but fair' wardens in hostels, Dunlop's (1980) 'firm and consistent policy', and Gelsthorpe and Morris' (1983:109) 'structured and firm setting'.
9   See also Sinclair's (1971) study of hostels where he noted that supervisors tended to determine who failed and who succeeded.

Enforcement of financial penalties

Mair and Lloyd (1989: 16) found that enforcement of Money Payment Supervision Orders (MPSOs) varied according to the circumstances of the offender, the style of the supervisor, and local policy or guidelines. There was enormous variation in enforcement practices, depending on how well MPSOs were integrated into mainstream probation work, and on fine enforcement approaches of different courts. Further, policy guidelines did not cover what type of enforcement methods should be used, rather they tended to concentrate on how to proceed once default had occurred.

Softley and Moxon (1982: 8-9) found promptness in taking initial action (and short intervals between follow up action) was the most important determinant of successful fine enforcement.[10] Those courts relying most heavily on means warrants were the least effective, since warrant execution took an average of six weeks. Teasdale (1989), like Softley and Moxon, also found that different courts had varying practices. However, none of the enforcement staff in Teasdale's 12 courts had information on which enforcement methods were the most effective.

Newburn (1988:43) found that fine enforcement officers were reluctant to use custody for default of compensation orders unless all other avenues had been tried. Both probation and fine enforcement officers had a degree of discretion over compensation order enforcement methods, which they used to their advantage to achieve payment. Simply going for early custody, which might be paralleled with early breach, would have reduced payment targets, and increased the burden on the criminal justice system.

Conclusion

With the exception of HMIP reports, most of the literature on the enforcement of community penalties was written before the 1992 NS were introduced and concentrates mainly on the CS orders. However, as this report will show, many of the issues raised remain relevant. First, there was considerable variation in enforcement practice, within and between probation areas. Second, there is little doubt that failures to attend received more enforcement attention than other types of failure to comply in all areas. Third, firm enforcement rules applied fairly appear most likely to result in successful completion of an order. Fourth, it would also seem that supervising officers see a potential conflict between adherence to formal

---

10 See also Home Office Working Group on Magistrates Courts (1982): NACRO report on fine default (1981).

enforcement policies on the one hand, and the use of professional judgement on the other. This might result in increased use of informal and unrecorded enforcement methods.

Finally, combination orders present three particular enforcement problems: variation in the types of offenders for which they are used; liaison difficulties between probation and CS officers; and, the greater leeway given by probation officers holding the order to offenders on the CS element of a combination order compared to offenders on straight CS orders.

3 Variations in the organisation of supervision and enforcement

Background

This chapter provides basic background information on the five probation services which participated in the study and outlines the similarities and differences in the way they organised supervision and formally enforced community orders.

As explained in Chapter One, the five areas in the study were chosen using Home Office Statistical Department data as a rough guide to different patterns of breach (whether breach led to the order being continued or revoked), and to ensure a mix of metropolitan, shire and other urban areas. Areas A and C were metropolitan boroughs with relatively high population density and inner city problems. Area B covered a small shire county, with a number of small towns and some rural patches. Areas D and E were chosen, partly, because they had a mix of urban and rural supervision.

Probation supervision

The organisation of probation supervision was very similar in all five areas. Senior probation officers headed generic teams of probation officers who directly managed all probation orders. These probation officers also 'held' combination orders, which meant supervising the probation component, liaising with the CS staff responsible for the other side of the order, and writing breach reports. There were also some specialist staff for intensive probation programmes, young offenders and women.

The main variation in the organisation of probation supervision and breach work was the extent to which specialist court and/or breach officers were available. Areas A, B and C had specialist court teams, who would, among other things, process breaches. Area B was unique, in that the court teams included specialist breach officers who were neither probation nor CS officers. In Area D, there were specialist court teams, but supervising officers would normally present their own breach cases in court. However, a specialist breach (probation) officer had recently been appointed in the major urban conurbation. In Area E, it was again the norm for rural probation officers to present their own breach cases, but a specialist breach (probation) officer had recently been appointed in the main urban area.

The research reviewed in Chapter Two suggested that at least some probation officers were unhappy with their dual roles of care and control when supervising an offender. However, in our study, none of the probation officers interviewed felt there was a dilemma for them in prosecuting an offender they were also supervising. *"Breaches would reinforce a good order, and if it was a bad order, there was no relationship to ruin anyway"* (SPO, Area D). Officers were more concerned that the use of specialist breach presentation officers might lead to the 'de-skilling' of supervising officers in the long run.

Community Service supervision

There was considerable variation in the extent to which SPOs and probation officers were involved in CS supervision and in the levels at which management functions were carried out. In Area A, CS staff were managed by three senior CS officers, who were supervised by a SPO. There were also specialist court CS officers who presented breach cases. In Area C, which was a much larger area, three SPOs managed area-based CS teams of probation and CS officers, court/breach officers and administrative staff. The probation officers managed groups of CS officers within each area. Community Service in Area E was centralised into one specialist team covering the whole probation service, and operating out of a single centre. A SPO and his deputy (probation officer) managed the four CS officers and four CS assistants. CS officers and assistants both supervised orders, but only CS officers presented breaches in court. CS assistants were more likely to carry out the bulk of site visits and following up absences with home visits.

In contrast, in Areas B and D, there was no supervision of CS orders by probation officers below the grade of ACPO. In Area B, all CS orders were the responsibility of a sole CS manager. Due to the size of this supervision task, there was a high level of devolved responsibility and decision making at CS officer level. The system was essentially the same in Area D, although CS orders here were run jointly by CS officers, project organisers and administration officers. CS officers dealt primarily with discipline interviews, writing breach reports, and breach presentation at court. Project organisers recorded attendance, and allocated offenders to placements. Administration officers were only marginally involved in enforcement, although they were expected to cross-question offenders who telephoned the office with explanations of absence. The HMIP thematic inspection of CS (HM Inspectorate of Probation, 1995a: 31) found it difficult to discern what specific contribution probation officers made which could not have been made by the experienced CS managers. This was largely true in our study, although welfare visits for offenders on CS in Area E were specifically referred to the probation officer working in the CS centre.

In all five areas, offenders working on placements were directly supervised by either full-time supervisors, part-time supervisors, or casual sessional supervisors (the latter worked without a contract, and were paid on an hourly basis). In most areas, some use was also made of individual placement supervisors. These were not directly employed by the probation service and usually worked for the agency with which the offender had been placed.

CS placements

The types of placements available on CS varied. In Areas A, C and E, there were three distinct types of placement. *Group* placements were used for the majority of offenders. Offenders selected for *individual* placements were selected for their low risk and reliability, which usually excluded offenders convicted of burglary, theft or fraud. *Workshops* were used for those who had special needs (e.g., physical or mental disabilities, single parents etc.), or where there were public safety considerations, for instance, for those convicted of violence or sex offences.

In all five areas, most offenders reported to a CS centre, from where they were allocated to a sessional supervisor. Attendance was nearly always recorded by a CS officer, or equivalent, limiting the enforcement scope of sessional workers to offenders' work performance and behaviour during CS sessions.

Occasionally, in some rural settings in Areas D and E, offenders reported directly to the work site, in which case sessional workers were then responsible for recording attendance and lateness. For all types of placement, sessional workers completed a report on each offender at the end of every work session, which was handed to the CS officer who held the order.

Enforcement during an order

Since the introduction of the 1992 NS, the formal approach to enforcement has been essentially the same for probation, CS and combination orders in all five areas. During an order, there was a system of three failures to comply before breach action was taken. The most common reason for breach was a build up of failures to attend. Following the first two failures to comply, the offender would receive warning letters. A third failure would normally result in breach and a return to court.

Both probation service staff and magistrates agreed that breaches involving other types of failure to comply (such as lateness for appointments or work sessions, failure to notify change of address, failure to comply with specific requirements of an order and threatening or troublesome behaviour) were relatively rare, and mainly occurred on CS orders.

Warning Letters

For failures to attend on probation orders, the enforcement systems were virtually identical in Areas A to D. A letter was sent out immediately asking for an explanation for the absence, and giving the date of the next appointment. These letters were increasingly severe, depending on the number of previous absences which were unacceptable, and finally threatened breach action. The letters were not standardised, and wording varied slightly depending on the probation officer's assessment of the offender. Any absence would be recorded on part C of the offender's case file, along with explanations, either acceptable or unacceptable. SPOs only expected to be consulted about a minority of breach cases where probation officers were unsure whether to proceed.

The system of warning letters for CS generally progressed in the same way, although these letters were standardised. Once breach action had been taken, offenders were normally informed that they were suspended from their current CS placements, although if they were willing to work pending the breach action, CS officers usually allowed this, and took their subsequent performance into account in any breach report recommendations to the court. In addition to recording failures to comply, sessional supervisors used a grading system for offenders which carried a record of motivation, work quality, effect on the other members of the group, etc. If the grade was poor, offenders could be temporarily suspended from the order subject to the outcome of an interview with a CS officer, where offenders were warned that if this poor performance continued, they would be breached.

Breach action

Under 1992 NS, if an offender failed to comply with an order three times within the space of six months,[1] and could not provide acceptable explanations, he or she would normally be breached. In all five areas, once the decision to breach an offender had been made, a probation and/or CS officer prepared a breach report.[2] This breach report usually contained a recommendation to the court for either a 'disciplinary breach' (i.e.,

---

1   Extended to 12 months under the current Standards.
2   Sometimes also called 'statement of facts'.

continuation of the order with a warning), or for revocation of the order and re-sentencing.[3]

All officers interviewed said they used disciplinary breaches where the intention was to reinforce respect for community penalties and to encourage the offender to comply with the terms of the order. They recommended revocation where an offender had effectively withdrawn his or her co-operation, or the order had become unworkable due to repeated poor attendance or personal circumstances.

Both probation and CS officers said that the majority of breaches for all types of community penalty were disciplinary in the first instance, but that recommendations for revocation became increasingly likely with successive breaches. If an offender did not attend from the beginning of an order, a recommendation for revocation was virtually automatic. However, available data do not entirely support these perceptions. Figures for England and Wales in 1994[4] suggest that 51 per cent of all breaches for CS orders resulted in continuation of the order, and 44 per cent ended in revocation. For probation orders, 59 per cent of all breaches resulted in revocation, and only 33 per cent in continuation. The same figures show a smaller proportion of offenders on probation orders were breached (9%) than of those on CS (24%) or combination orders (22%). Taken together, these figures rather undermine probation officers' claims that they are most likely to use breach action constructively, but lend some support to the similar claims of CS officers.

If offenders were permitted to continue a community order after breach action, they generally started afresh, and were allowed up to three further failures to comply before breach action was taken a second time. However, on CS orders in Area D, offenders were generally allowed only one more failure to comply before being breached again. Revocation and re-sentencing could result in a different community sentence, a fine, custody or a discharge.

Use of local guidelines

Under both 1992 (pp.43-44, 77) and 1995 (p.3) National Standards, probation services are expected to produce local guidelines for all aspects of NS, including enforcement and breach procedures. All five services had done so, although these varied in form and content.

---

3   Revocation is not always the result of breach action, and can be recommended for good progress, or in the 'interests of justice' e.g., due to ill health, gaining full time employment (which can make CS unworkable in some cases), because the offender had been given a custodial sentence at another court appearance, etc.
4   See Annex III.

Generally, probation service staff handbooks covered the preparation of breach cases and prosecution. In Areas A and C, the probation service and clerks from all of the local courts had developed a breach prosecution manual. In Area A, all probation officers interviewed knew of the local breach prosecution manual and could bring it to hand easily. This was also true of all specialist breach/court officers in Area C, although not all supervising probation officers were aware of the manual. Some probation officers in Area A referred to memos regarding enforcement issues circulated as problems occurred, although most of them did not have the memos to hand.

In Area B, local guidelines consisted of a breach policy statement and handbook, with separate sections for supervising officers and court (breach prosecution) officers. The service policy was to breach on the second failure to comply (i.e., it was more restrictive than NS), unless agreed otherwise with a SPO. However, in practice, probation officers would nearly always allow three failures to comply (in tune with NS), unless the offender had not attended from the outset. Specialist breach prosecution officers in Area B also had a job description which set out the breach process in detail. The community supervision ACPO in Area B explained that there was no information for probation or CS officers in the local guidelines on how to decide whether rules had been broken. This was left to professional judgement. She had also issued occasional memos on local enforcement practice, but these were the result of recurrent discussions, otherwise *"what I see is so hit and miss, I can't send out memos on single incidents."*

Only Area D had produced a comprehensive enforcement policy document, covering all aspects of ensuring compliance during an order and the breach process. This document was largely determined by the findings of a 1994 internal inspection of combination orders. This inspection had revealed that probation officers were unclear about what was an acceptable absence and what was not. As a result, enforcement was given a higher profile and an 'Enforcement Policy' document was developed, which covered practical enforcement issues for both probation and CS orders – *"Although the Standards are very explicit, there are areas where guidance is needed. What is an acceptable and what is an unacceptable absence for instance"* (ACPO).[5] A first draft of a more detailed 'Enforcement Policy' paper had also been prepared. This draft covered all aspects of enforcement, from the importance of clear PSRs, induction, initial appointments, following up non-attendance, warning letters, recording practices, a detailed breach section, and post-breach supervision.

---

5   The enforcement policy document contained a list of criteria by which the acceptability of explanations should be judged. These included: the source of the explanation; the nature of the evidence; the pattern of previous failures; offenders' maturity and/or lifestyle; and any special needs, such as gender or religion.

Local guidelines for breach preparation and prosecution for CS orders were essentially the same as for probation orders. However, there was noticeably more coverage of enforcement issues prior to breach action, including how to deal with threats to sessional supervisors, sending offenders home, and intimidation or racist comments to other offenders. For example, offenders using mobile telephones during CS work was cited as an increasing problem in Areas C, D and E, and memos had been issued making it 'a failure to comply' on the grounds of 'failing to work as directed'. One offender had already been breached for this in Area E.

Each CS office in Area C had its own handbook which covered how National Standards and other aspects of the work should be implemented. A training video had been produced for sessional supervisors which included advice on running groups and dealing with difficult situations. Each senior probation officer in CS held a policy file with a complete (and up-to-date) set of the services policies. Areas B and C had also produced handbooks, including enforcement issues for sessional workers. In the other areas, sessional workers based their enforcement practice on the rules leaflet given to offenders, plus any on-the-job instruction given by CS officers.

Summary

The main findings on how the supervision and enforcement of community orders was organised can be summarised as follows.

- Probation supervision teams were organised along broadly similar lines throughout all five areas. However, the extent to which probation officers were involved in CS supervision, and enforcement, varied considerably.

- The extent to which offenders on CS orders were allocated to individual, group or workshop placements varied considerably across the five areas.

- Formally, offenders were allowed a maximum of three failures to comply before breach action was taken. Most of these failures were said by CS and probation officers to be attendance-related.

- Once breach action had been taken, both CS and probation officers made recommendations to the court about whether the order ought to continue or be revoked. All officers said that in the first instance, they were most likely to recommend continuation, although available data do not entirely support this view for probation orders.

- Local guidelines generally concentrated on preparation of breach cases and prosecution. Only one area had developed a comprehensive policy which covered enforcement issues prior to breach action.

4 Enforcement practice: issues and problems

There are two relatively distinct aspects to enforcement practice: ensuring compliance during an order; and taking breach action. If supervising officers are able to promote compliance successfully, they will be able to avoid the need for breach action. This chapter examines issues and practices in ensuring compliance, while Chapter Five covers breach action and the court process.

Discretion and National Standards

Although this was not a study of compliance with National Standards, it was important to establish supervising officers' views on the relationship between discretion and the Standards, before considering their enforcement practices. As stated above, interviews took place in three of the five areas in the study before the introduction of the new Standards in March 1995. Interviews were carried out after the publication of the new Standards in March 1995, but prior to their implementation, in the other two areas.

ACPOs and SPOs interviewed stressed that NS formed part of probation officers' training, and therefore that *"newer officers coming in have less problems with National Standards. Some of the older ones are having to make leaps to catch up, but it's not like when you used to have individual officers who didn't believe in breach"* (SPO, Area A). In fact, National Standards were generally welcomed by both probation and CS officers in all five areas, as a way of ensuring consistent enforcement practice. Some went further, arguing that the 1992 Standards had introduced existing good practice to all officers, and that they were happy with the degree of flexibility allowed under the Standards. One SPO in Area E added that without NS, enforcement would now be chaotic.

Generally, probation and CS officers were happy with the extent to which the 1992 National Standards allowed supervisors to exercise professional judgement. Only two SPOs and two probation officers expressed concern that the 1992 NS had cut down the level of discretion in enforcing probation orders. However, all probation officers and SPOs stressed that the inclusion of words such as 'reasonable', 'should', or, 'may' in the Standards were helpful since they allowed room for professional interpretation. CS officers generally agreed that they needed to exercise professional judgement only in a few instances, whereas probation officers tended to stress the need for professional discretion and interpretation of National Standards for nearly all cases. The community supervision ACPO interviewed in Area B argued *"I don't have a problem with the current arrangements, but you can't mechanise a chaotic individual. At the end of the day, you have to make individual judgements."*

All probation and CS officers agreed that NS had reduced the variability of treatment of offenders, and that enforcement was now fairer. The following comment was typical of probation officers' responses – *"I think overall it's achieved a … degree of fairness, but I still think you can operate a general system of fairness and allow a degree of discretion"* (SPO, Area E).

All probation officers who had pre-NS experience thought that the Standards had increased the number of breaches. However, they also thought that breaches were now used more constructively towards achieving successful completion of the order. Nearly all CS officers agreed with this, although two, from different areas, thought that the Standards had not changed their previous enforcement methods.

In general, probation officers exercised more discretion than CS officers, although in part, this was due to the different demands of probation and CS orders. Most probation officers stressed the need for a concrete objective in breaching an offender: as one officer put it – *"If they've had their chance and were never seriously interested in taking it, I think it's quite right they should be breached and re-sentenced to some alternative"* (Probation Officer, Area E). However, they also identified cases where the strict application of NS was not appropriate – *"If you have an addict who is trying to undertake rehabilitation, just by the nature of the lifestyle, they're going to be unreliable. You could actually get yourself a well motivated offender … who, in the course of negotiating [drug rehabilitation] with their probation officer, may miss three or four appointments … then you've suddenly got breach proceedings intruding on a therapeutic process. Breach might have satisfied the requirements of the law, but in the long term, you haven't prevented people offending."* (Probation Officer, Area E). Of course, both 1992 and 1995 NS allow for discretion in exceptional cases. However, the latter have attempted to improve accountability by removing words such as 'reasonable', 'should' and 'may' and inciting that supervising officers consult their line managers before exercising discretion.

Although less discretion was exercised on CS orders, all CS officers agreed that it was important. As one full-time supervisor in Area D put it, *"If you started judging them on everything they said to you that day, you could send them all off at ten o' clock in the morning. You have to step back and monitor the situation".*

Comments on the 1995 National Standards

In Areas A, B and C, only seven probation and CS officers had seen the 'near final draft' of the 1995 NS. These officers generally saw the new Standards as more restrictive. Senior probation and CS officers commented that if the new NS were unrealistic, they might ignore them in practice, and continue applying the 1992 Standards. Probation and CS officers in Area B thought that the tighter 1995 Standards might lead them to extend their professional judgement further – *"You can either tighten up and become a production line, or use more benefit of the doubt to effectively stay the same"* (CS Officer).

Interviews in Areas D and E took place between May and September 1995, after the new NS had been published (although they had not yet been implemented in these areas). Roughly half of the probation and CS staff in Area D, and all in Area E (except sessional workers) had seen the new Standards. Of these, half thought that the new breach rules meant that an offender should be returned to court after a maximum of two failures to comply, rather than after a maximum of three as intended. Magistrates were equally confused in Areas D and E. Six of the eight magistrates interviewed in these two areas thought that breach proceedings should commence after a maximum of two failures to comply. In fact, only the wording has changed, and the maximum number of failures to comply remains unchanged at three, (for example see Home Office 1992, 40 cf. Home Office 1995c, 22).

None of the probation officers interviewed supported the extension of the breach accounting period from six to twelve months – *"somebody could get back on course and then they could have a subsequent lapse, so you would only be allowed one additional warning in twelve months."* (SPO).

Methods of ensuring compliance

Probation and CS officers employed several strategies throughout the five areas, to minimise failures to comply, and, ultimately, the need to breach.

If offenders, who were part way through a probation order, started to miss appointments, supervising officers in all five areas sometimes put offenders on weekly rather than monthly reporting, effectively increasing the number of appointments. The reasoning behind this was typically as follows – *"If they start to mess about, you put them on fortnightly reporting, and they then have double the chance of fulfiling their attendance for the month"* (Probation Officer, Area E). However, other probation officers in the same area argued that changing the reporting cycle in this way might also double offenders' chances of failing to attend.

CS officers sometimes cancelled the hours worked in a session where an offender had been difficult. In Area D, this was commonly used for young offenders who were 'messing about' as a group, and only if *"no-one was hurt and nothing was damaged"* (CS Officer). In Area B, where a generally compliant offender had technically breached an order through three failures to attend, the CS officer and breach officer sometimes agreed to seek a date for the breach hearing after the projected end of the order (assuming all of the hours were completed on time). This offered an incentive to an offender not to incur a further failure to comply, and if the order were successfully completed, the breach proceedings were withdrawn.

Most SPOs encouraged probation officers to revoke orders early for good progress. SPOs thought that this was an incentive to offenders to comply with an order, but it was also used to reduce high caseloads. However, in the long run, this may have a negative effect, as the quality of the progress made by the offender may become a secondary consideration to the desire to reduce officer workload.

Most officers thought that getting offenders to notify them in advance of likely absences was a positive enforcement tool, which encouraged offenders to actively co-operate with the terms of their order. All probation officers were likely to accept a notification or request from an offender for permission to be absent, provided these were not too frequent. Professional judgement and previous knowledge of an offender were seen as important here – *"It is what they are saying, and how reliable or consistent they have been in the past. You know whether people are bullshitting or conning you"* (Probation Officer, Area E). For these reasons, there tended to be less leniency at the beginning of an order, or with a previously unknown offender.

For CS, the situation varied between areas. In Area A, CS officers operated a similar system to probation officers – *"I stress making contact – telephoning and telling me why – if they ask in advance, they know whether I will allow a day off with permission and that's perfectly acceptable"* (CS officer). In Area B, CS officers would accept an isolated incident without evidence, but only if the offender suggested making up the lost time. In Areas C, D and E, advanced warning of absence was viewed favourably – *"at least if they're phoning up they're letting you know what's happening and it goes some way to understanding them, and to what action to take after that"* (CS Assistant, Area E). However, proof for that absence was always requested on the next work date.

None of the five areas studied had set up a formal appointment card or diary system for offenders on probation orders. However, these were sometimes used by individual probation officers. These officers stressed that appointment cards were only useful for some offenders. For those with chaotic lifestyles, probation officers felt that appointment cards were likely to be lost, and they employed other methods. For instance, in the urban centre of Area D, offenders were often asked to report on the day they also signed for social security payments. In Area E, one probation officer kept offenders whose lives were particularly chaotic (e.g., drug misusers) on fortnightly reporting - *"I find that if I leave it for any longer than a fortnight I've lost them"* (Probation Officer, Area E). Appointment cards were not considered necessary for offenders on CS orders, since they always received written confirmation of their next work date at the end of each work session.

Variation in CS placement allocation and supervision

As outlined in Chapter Three, offenders on CS orders were allocated to one of three types of placement: individual, group and workshop. Group and workshop placements were directly supervised by paid sessional supervisors, whereas individual placements were generally supervised either by staff from another agency, or by individual 'beneficiaries' (for instance, where an offender carries out tasks for an elderly person). However, the proportionate allocation of offenders to these different types of placement varied between areas. The most striking contrast was between Areas B and D.

Area B ran some workshops, but allocated most offenders initially into group placements. If offenders performed well in these groups, they were considered for individual placements. In fact, the area CS policy was to put as many offenders as possible on individual placements to reduce the cost of supervision.

In contrast, CS officers in Area D put greater emphasis on the quality of supervision and enforcement than on the relative cost of different types of placement. As a result, the majority of offenders on CS orders were supervised by sessional workers on group placements. Individual placements had been used more extensively in the past, but became unpopular with all CS staff because of the poor quality of enforcement by individual supervisors. Individual placements and workshops were now limited to use for offenders with special requirements (such as sex offenders, single parents and disabled offenders).

Indeed, the concept of supervision on individual placements varied widely. In Area C, named individual placement supervisors were responsible for offenders, but in Area B, the concept of individual supervision (at one office) was very broad - *"We don't have individual supervisors. The only individual placements we have are for those who can be trusted on their own. There is no responsible person, just whoever is on duty that day. We would visit during the course of the day, but they are not closely supervised"* (CS Officer). Even for group work, supervision was not always consistent. For instance, in Area B, a CS officer noted that offenders were regularly dropped off in a wood with their equipment, and their performance was judged on *"what had happened to the woods when they were picked up"*!

There was also some evidence, in Areas B and D, of the type of inappropriate 'contract' between offenders and sessional workers that Vass (1989) described.[1] Three supervisors at one CS office in Area D were described by the CS officer and project organiser as 'nightmares' - *"They didn't come. When they came, they couldn't supervise and the work they turned out was atrocious"* (project organiser). As a result of the lax attitude to hours and discipline, the quality of enforcement and supervision had been generally poor. In Area B, one sessional worker had also been clocking off early and giving the offenders extra hours. This was only detected when offenders expressed surprise at the number of hours they had completed. Further, CS officers and sessional workers in Areas B and D were increasingly employed on short term contracts. The CS manager in Area B thought that this increasing insecurity was reducing the CS staff's motivation and willingness to enforce orders strictly.

One practice was identified which was common to group placements in all areas. Known 'difficult offenders' were allocated to different groups. In Area B, troublesome behaviour on individual placements, was tackled by moving the offender to group work, to ensure more rigorous supervision, and (if this failed) to make it easier to collect evidence of failures to comply.

All sessional workers were required to assess an offender's performance, in a short report for CS officers, at the end of each work session. Details of grading systems varied between areas, but usually indicated whether work and attitude had been satisfactory. A poor performance marking usually resulted in an informal verbal warning from the CS officer, or in more serious cases, it was recorded as a failure to comply.

Discretion

Both probation and CS officers were more likely to use the above discretionary enforcement methods with a generally compliant offender who

---

1 See Chapter Two.

was nearing the end of an order – *"You'd have to think quite carefully about what you were writing down as being an acceptable and an unacceptable absence, and I guess that people who had previously shown a great commitment to the order would be encouraged and nursed and given lots more opportunity"* (SPO, Area A). In Areas D and E, this also was justified, partly, on the grounds of limited resources – *"In reality, if they're within three months of the end of the order and they've not been in trouble or re-offended, you would tend not to want to enforce the order to the extreme, so you'd look at telephone contact, 'you come in and see me if it's a problem', or use the 'reporting centre'. You tend not to want face to face contact towards the end, because you've got new people starting orders who you've got to see once a week"* (Probation Officer, Area D).

Because of the time and cost involved in breaching offenders, magistrates were in favour of these informal methods in certain circumstances, typically – *"where an offender has completed most of the order but then gets de-mob happy, I would have a lot of sympathy for changing his reporting pattern to pull him up before considering breach. Nobody wants to go back to square one. He's worked out 80 to 90% of his punishment – it seems a common sense way of dealing with it. I think National Standards have cut that down to a degree"* (Chairman of community penalties subcommittee, Area A). Interestingly, in Area D, two magistrates who were presented with a breach near the end of a probation order thought it was the norm to revoke the order with no further penalty![2]

Enforcing failures to comply

Most of the above methods were designed to prevent failures to comply with an order. However, there was a clear contrast between probation and CS officers in the amount of leeway given, before the decision was taken to record a failure to comply.

Failures to attend

Failures to attend, as noted, formed the vast majority of failures to comply. They were much more rigorously recorded by CS officers than by most probation order supervisors. Offenders were expected to attend the CS office, usually by nine o' clock in the morning, and marking attendance was usually the responsibility of a CS officer. In Areas A to D, CS offenders were generally allowed to be between 10 and 15 minutes late, according to fixed

---

2   See Annex III. In 1994, 7 per cent of probation order breaches, 5 per cent of CS order breaches, and 2 per cent of combination order breaches resulted in discharges.

local policies. After this time, a failure to attend was recorded, and the offender was not allowed to work that day. Lateness in Area D also incurred a penalty of 15 minutes, deducted from the hours already worked. By contrast, the amount of leeway for lateness in Area E was left to the discretion of the supervisor. One commented that *"if they are sort of half an hour late without good reason you'd start thinking about saying 'look sorry, it's not good enough', but again, it's a little flexible."* This would seem to support Pease and West's (1977) argument that CS is enforced unevenly between different probation services.

There was much less emphasis on punctuality for probation orders. If an offender failed a probation appointment, but was able to come in the same week, the probation officers interviewed, in all five areas, tended to accept this and did not record a failure to attend. Indeed, an internal inspection team in Area D had already noted – *"Not only did probation officers have a more liberal attitude to what constituted an acceptable excuse, but in many cases they did not seem even to think in these terms".*[3]

Other failures to comply

Probation officers and CS staff dealt differently with 'troublesome' or 'unco-operative' offenders. If offenders would not address their offending behaviour or otherwise engage with their supervisors in probation sessions, probation officers, particularly in Areas D and E, argued that enforcement was difficult, due to the wording of the probation orders[4] – *"You don't tend to get very many of the 'unco-operative' breaches now because you haven't got that sort of discretion. You see, the order used to cater for them being badly behaved [before CJA 1991]. The order used to say 'you've got to be of good behaviour'. If you gave them instructions not to be abusive when they came here you could breach them"* (SPO, Area E).

This sort of view had led to the use of a 'low grade reporting' system for difficult offenders in Areas D and E. This system had originally been introduced to cater for offenders who had made good progress, but who were not yet eligible for early revocation (and these offenders still formed the bulk of those on low grade reporting).

In Area E, offenders on such a system reported to a duty assistant (PSO ancillary grade) at the probation office, and in Area D, they reported to a probation officer at the probation day centre (referred to as the 'reporting

---

3   The 1994 HMIP thematic Inspection of CS (p.38) noted a recording rate of 79 per cent for non-compliance. The internal inspection of combination orders in Area D noted an equivalent recording rate for CS of 87 per cent, but only 25 per cent for probation!

4   See Ward and Ward (1993: 102-103) and Stone (1994: 32).

centre' in this context). In all low grade reporting cases, offenders were asked to sign an attendance register,[5] and they could request an interview with their supervising officer at any time. Failures to attend were subject to the normal breach procedures. SPOs and probation officers in these two areas also commented that they were increasingly using this system as a way of managing high caseloads. Since most failures to comply with probation orders amounted to failures to attend, it is arguable that offenders were just as likely to breach the order under this system as they were if they were subject to direct supervision. However, the absence of any further supervision of the offender questions the purpose of a probation order disposal.

Due to the different nature of CS orders, it is not surprising that CS officers had developed a rather different system of dealing with troublesome behaviour. Sessional supervisors admitted that there could be a build-up of difficult behaviour during an order, or even in a single session, which required a level of toleration because the individual incidents were not sufficiently serious to record a failure to work as directed – essentially an informal system of enforcement. Offenders would be allowed up to three 'warnings' per work session before being sent home and a failure to comply recorded. Alternatively, workers could be transferred from an interesting project, e.g. decorating, to a more tedious and physically demanding project. *"When they complain about the digging, you say 'we tried you on painting, we tried you on joinery, and you made a mess of it – now when you learn to comply, you'll get better work' "* (project organiser, Area D). The sessional supervisors and the project organisers operated a level of discretion in deciding which method was likely to be effective.

Failures to comply on probation orders with requirements

Where offenders were on a probation order with additional requirements, probation officers tended to breach them for not turning up, rather than for refusing to fully participate when they did attend. However, breach for poor participation was more likely on requirements run by probation service staff, such as intensive probation programmes, or probation centres, than when the probation service had no direct control over the requirement. For instance, four probation officers noted that there were occasional problems with staff at drug rehabilitation units and psychiatrists, who were not prepared to inform supervising officers about the performance, or occasionally, even the attendance of offenders.

---

5   It is questionable whether this practice is in line with the current Standards (see Home Office, 1995c:22), which state that "The signing of a register by the offender without any contact with supervising staff, *or staff operating under their direction*, should not count towards the completion of the order." (Emphasis added.) On the one hand, this may rule out low grade reporting; on the other hand it may endorse it, if 'staff operating under [supervising staff's] direction' is interpreted broadly.

Many probation requirements were organised as rolling programmes which allowed offenders to attend as soon as they started their orders. However, some programmes had definite start dates, with each session building on the previous one. These types of programmes could cause particular enforcement dilemmas. For instance, if offenders missed the first appointment of their requirement, they would not be able to join the following sessions. However, if they were attending their probation appointments, it was difficult to classify this type of non-attendance as wilful. Decisions on whether to breach offenders in this position were made on a case by case basis in regular meetings of the community supervision teams, and would partly depend on whether the offender could complete the next available programme within the period of their probation order.

Home visits

As the literature review in Chapter Two makes clear, Drakeford (1993) suggested that supervising officers should routinely make home visits in all cases where breach action was being considered. However, neither probation, nor CS officers interviewed used home visits in this way. In Areas A to D, CS home visits were only occasional and were usually to check on sickness, working hours, or in rare cases, family welfare issues. *"Where somebody says I work from seven o'clock in the morning to ten at night, I've been known to knock on their door at eight o'clock to see if they're in"* (CS officer, Area D). In Area E, CS officers made more regular home visits for the same reasons, and in the few cases where there were welfare concerns, these were referred to the managing probation officer to carry out a further visit.

For probation orders in urban areas, home visits were rare. Most officers said this was because they lacked the time to carry out such visits due to their heavy caseloads. In rural areas, home visits were often used in place of appointments at a probation office – *"because it's a vast area with a small number of officers and no transport. They actually have the highest compliance rate in the entire county, surprise, surprise"* (ACPO, Area D). At the rural office in Area E, the probation officer thought that home visits were no guarantee of better attendance. He made firm appointment times, and if the offender was not there, he recorded this as a failure to comply. Since offenders in his area were more likely to live with their families, he sometime asked relatives to use their influence to ensure the offender's compliance in future.

Most officers stressed the need for health and safety considerations on home visits. Women supervisors, in particular, mentioned the dangers in some urban areas of visiting a previously unknown offender, or of returning to a parked car that had been tampered with or broken into.

The follow-up process in Area E

The enforcement process for failures to attend in Area E was unusual, and for this reason is covered in some detail here. In the major urban area of this probation service, a full-time follow-up officer (PSO ancillary grade) was employed to visit all those offenders on probation orders who failed to keep their appointments. As more probation officers were made aware of the follow-up service, the number of referrals grew,[5] and, at the time this study was carried out, probation managers were discussing funding for a further full time follow-up officer who would also cover some of the rural areas.

On an offender's first failure to attend, probation officers referred the case to the follow-up officer who would take a first (standardised) warning letter to the offender's last known address to make enquiries and, where possible, obtain an explanation. These referrals took place immediately with all probation orders where the offender had not arrived for his/her first appointment. If an order was partly completed and had been relatively unproblematic, probation officers sometimes waited for offenders' explanations at their next appointments, rather than referring them immediately to the follow-up officer. However, for all second failures to comply, referrals were nearly always made immediately.

Conversely, if offenders moved to another local address without informing their probation officer, but had continued to attend their orders, this was technically a failure to notify change of address for which they could be breached. However, the follow-up officer argued that this was often associated with a chaotic lifestyle more than wilful non-compliance. In these circumstances he reported the new address to the probation officer, who, for the same reasons, rarely took breach action.

The follow-up officer was responsible for recording an offender's explanation for his/her failure to attend, but the acceptability of that explanation was judged by the supervising probation officer. Neither the follow-up officer, nor probation officers, saw his role as replacing home visits, but some of the information he gathered on offenders' circumstances was useful to probation officers. If an offender was known to be potentially violent, another PSO accompanied the follow-up officer.

The follow-up officer had built up a level of investigative expertise and local contacts in his previous job as a police constable. However, his investigative tasks were mainly limited to visiting an offender's last known address and contacting neighbours to get as much information as possible. Some

---

6   From 1 January to 22 August 1995 he had made 1,174 visits to home addresses, an average of about 35 per week.

explanations required further investigation, e.g. checking on hospital admissions, but partly because of the size of the officer's caseload, and partly because he felt this went beyond his brief, he did not pursue investigations which involved the DSS or housing agencies.

Interviews with probation officers and the breach officer in this area suggested that solicitors were challenging breaches on evidential technicalities more frequently than in other areas in the study (see Chapter Five). Because of this, the follow-up officer now insisted that offenders, or their families, sign a pro forma to certify that they had received their warning letters and summonses. If the offender was not at home, the follow-up officer would get a member of the family to sign the receipt. However, he explained that it was more difficult to do this where the offender lived alone in rented accommodation, without making it known that the offender was on probation. If there was no reply, a warning letter was left at the address, and a copy also sent by first class post, both of which were recorded by the follow-up officer, who could then attend court as a witness if the failure to comply were challenged.

The effectiveness of the follow-up officer was not being monitored at the time this research was conducted. However, the officer pointed out that the follow-up method ensured prompt enforcement action which was important for the successful completion of probation orders, especially *"if we have a person who has a problem. I can locate them very quickly and get them to come in, and it seems to work. I always get them to ring now or get them to go down the office"*. He also thought that failures to attend were tackled much more quickly than before his post had been created – *"I try to do same day delivery, nearly always within 24 hours."*

Combination orders

Three specific enforcement issues for combination orders emerged from our interviews, and were consistent with the studies by Moloney (1995), Mair et al. (1994), Lloyd (1994) and with findings from Area D's 1994 internal inspection of combination orders. These were: probation and CS officers thought that magistrates did not always follow PSR proposals, and this could result in combination orders being used inappropriately; liaison problems between probation and CS officers on the different components of the order; and the greater leeway allowed by probation officers than by CS officers.

Unsuitable offenders and PSRs

The 1992 NS anticipated that the majority of combination orders would come from the Crown Court, but in practice, most were made out by magistrates.[6] Probation officers in Areas A, B and C thought that magistrates made out more combination orders than were proposed. They were concerned that this sometimes resulted in unsuitable offenders attempting to complete combination orders (e.g., chaotic drug misusers), thus incurring high breach and revocation rates.[7] They also claimed that, on re-sentencing, these offenders often received the probation or CS orders that probation officers had originally proposed, rather than custody. Both probation and senior CS officers felt that the entire process, from the original sentence, through to revocation and re-sentencing, was unnecessarily wasteful of resources.

All but three of the 19 magistrates interviewed had some sympathy with this point of view. They observed that JPs with longer service and who had not served on community penalties committees often did not regard a probation order as a punishment. As a result, they sometimes added a CS component to a proposal for a probation order, as a way of ensuring that the offender made some reparation to the community through physical work. In doing so however, these magistrates often failed to take account of the fact that chaotic offenders would have difficulty in working under strict conditions, and were therefore likely to be breached very quickly.

In contrast, probation officers in Areas D and E were more confident that both magistrates and probation officers had a better understanding of the issues involved in proposing and sentencing offenders to combination orders. They felt that probation officers in these areas were more likely to propose a combination order, or state why one was unsuitable. In addition, PSR writers in Area E made referrals to CS officers for serious offences and/or where the offender appeared to have a chaotic lifestyle. In such circumstances, CS staff supplied a statement suggesting whether an offender was suitable for a combination order or not – *"That's cut back on a lot of people getting CS. I mean, we put it in the [pre-sentence] report 'not suitable for CS', and magistrates don't go against it"* (SPO, Area E). The magistrates interviewed in Area E confirmed this.

Some SPOs in all areas, although agreeing that magistrates were often to blame for sentencing unsuitable offenders to combination orders, said that PSR writers could also contribute to the problem. Consistent with an

---

7   See Annex IV, and Mair et al., 1994.
8   For England and Wales in 1994, the breach ratio for combination orders was 22.4 per cent, just under that of CS orders, but with a much higher revocation rate at 73 per cent. See Annex III.

internal inspection in Area D, these SPOs noted that combination orders for unsuitable offenders could sometimes be the result of unclear PSR proposals or because probation officers rarely stated that combination orders were inappropriate in PSRs. Indeed, the internal inspection found that, of all cases where combination orders were made but not explicitly proposed in Area D, 27 per cent of PSRs had only a tentative proposal, and 40 per cent of proposals for probation orders had assessed the offender as also suitable for CS. To the inspection team, this seemed *"a virtual invitation to the courts to make a Combination Order, and showed once more the need for a firm, clear proposal"*.

SPOs in Area D argued that they were still receiving some 'mixed grill' PSRs, especially where the court had requested that 'all options be explored', and a SPO in Area B had had to intervene on a number of occasions to ask for clearer PSRs to be written.[8] All magistrates interviewed preferred PSRs with clear proposals, and thought this had improved since the introduction of NS. However, they also thought that their confidence in community penalties would be improved if probation officers recommended combination orders, or custody more often.

Liaison between probation and CS staff

There was evidence that probation and CS liaison on combination orders was problematic in all five areas in the study. The internal inspection in Area D noted that there was far more communication from CS to probation officers than the other way round. This view was also confirmed, without exception, by all probation officers interviewed in Area D, and with only three exceptions in all other areas. Probation officers generally expected to be told about failures to comply on the CS element, but did not see the need to similarly inform CS staff of failures to comply on the probation element.[9] As one probation officer in Area E put it – *"What do they need to know for. They'd only try to breach them faster. They aren't building up a social work picture"!* The internal inspection in Area D recommended that probation managers should monitor the recording of failures to comply between the two components of the order, but there was no evidence of this happening from our interviews with SPOs in any area.

Allowing extra leeway

With the exception of Area B, CS staff complained that probation officers

---

9   Mair et al. (1994:18, 27, 31-32) also found some evidence of this.
10   The 1992 NS (p. 83) state that *"If different people are supervising the order, they should be in touch with each other prior to the commencement of breach proceedings."*

often allowed extra leeway to offenders on combination orders, which resulted in uneven enforcement between those on straight CS orders and those on combination orders – *"The problem is that you can end up with people who are subject to CS orders, who have different standards applied to them"* (Senior CS Officer, Area A). CS officers consistently complained that probation officers were less rigorous than them, in accepting proof of explanations of absence *"They are keen to accept excuses, reasons for absence, that we don't necessarily consider are sensible"* (CS officer, Area C). In turn, CS officers thought this had a negative effect for discipline and morale on CS orders.

In Area B, there were no similar complaints from CS officers, and although probation officers expected to discuss a combination order case before breach action was taken, none thought it was his/her role to intervene. The CS manager confirmed this view – *"I'm not involved in too many cases where the CS officer thinks the probation officer has backed off breach. There are the odd one or two...the bulk has been with Youth Justice"*.

In contrast to the other four areas, CS officers in Area B also prepared the breach report for combination orders if the breach was on their side of the order. The specialist breach officers would then prosecute the breach on direct instructions from CS officers. In the other four areas, probation officers took CS officers' views into account in breach reports, but the CS officers often felt that they were not given enough weight. In Area D, an attempt had been made to rectify this problem. If the CS officer did not agree with the breach recommendation, or felt other points should be added, these views had to be incorporated into the breach presentation at court. However, most probation and CS officers felt that this rather public disagreement was damaging to the image of community penalties in general, and for magistrates' confidence in enforcement in particular.

Monitoring and supervision

All five areas carried out regular service-wide monitoring exercises on probation and CS orders, although time frames (from monthly to six-monthly) and sampling frames (from one-in-three to one-in-six cases) varied. These exercises were for headquarters' staff to measure, among other things, area enforcement performance against NS and key performance indicators, and were generally based on forms or questionnaires filled out and returned by SPOs.

The 13 SPOs who had responsibility for the enforcement of probation orders said they rarely requested sight of the service-wide monitoring information, and preferred to rely on two office-based methods.

The first of these involved probation officers bringing problematic cases to regular supervision team meetings. The weakness of this approach is that seniors are only aware of problems if probation officers choose to bring them to their attention (see McWilliams and Pease, 1990; Humphrey and Pease, 1992; Burnett, 1996). Indeed, the SPOs interviewed could recall few cases where probation officers were deliberately resisting breach action. However, they argued that their second monitoring method, caseload scrutinies, would pick up any undisclosed problems. These were carried out by SPOs, usually every six months. Again, sampling methods varied depending on the size of the supervision caseload. New probation officers' cases were scrutinised more closely and more often.

Monitoring of CS orders was computerised in all five areas, allowing CS managers to make any number of ad hoc checks on the supervision and enforcement of CS orders. CS managers tended to carry out a six-monthly scrutiny of a sample of cases which were then examined in detail. These scrutinies were used to identify ways in which to improve the performance of both individual supervisors, and the CS unit generally. For example, the scrutiny in Area E had shown that although CS staff were checking up on the reasons for absences, these were not always recorded on the offenders' files.[10] In addition, CS managers in Areas B to E also had regular one-to-one supervision sessions with CS officers to discuss individual case files.

The overall impression of the monitoring and supervision of the enforcement of community penalties in all five areas matched the findings of the internal inspection in Area D. CS managers were able to draw on a largely computerised monitoring system and were generally well organised. The supervision of probation enforcement was generally not computerised and therefore depended more on the personal efficiency of individual SPOs. This contrast was freely admitted in our interviews, and SPOs commented that it was easier to build a monitoring system for CS, as the work was inherently more straightforward.

CS staff training

None of the CS officers and sessional workers who were interviewed had received any formal training. All initial instruction, including enforcement training, was received on-the-job. General training on issues such as anti-discriminatory practice and health and safety, had now been introduced for new CS officers, but with no specific enforcement input. All CS officers and managers thought that formal training was an increasingly important issue,

---

11   This was also found to be the case elsewhere in the country by HM Inspectorate of Probation – see Home Office, 1995a: 38

because their jobs had changed, from what the CS manager in Area B described as a 'jack-of-all-trades', to caseload managers. There were plans in Areas B and E to introduce one-day training sessions for CS officers run by the specialist breach officers.

Group and workshop sessional workers generally thought that on-the-job training was adequate for the limited enforcement functions they performed. However, individual placement supervisors received neither formal nor on-the-job enforcement training. Area C had recently produced a training video for sessional workers, which included advice on running groups and dealing with difficult offenders.

Summary

The main findings from this chapter are presented below.

- In general, probation and CS officers thought that the 1992 Standards had improved consistency of enforcement practice, while leaving adequate provision for the use of discretion. However, probation officers were less complimentary about the 1995 Standards and thought that they attempted to restrict discretion too much.

- Probation officers were most likely to use their discretion not to record lateness or missed appointments as failures to comply when dealing with offenders who had particularly chaotic lifestyles.

- Some probation officers dealt with missed appointments by putting the offender on a more frequent reporting cycle (but others saw this as doubling an offender's opportunity to fail to comply). CS officers sometimes sent offenders home, and cancelled the hours they had worked in that session, instead of breaching them. Magistrates were generally in favour of these informal methods.

- The use of appointment cards or diaries was seen as good practice by some probation officers, and offenders on CS orders always received written confirmation of their next work date at the end of each work session. However, probation officers thought such cards were unlikely to be effective for offenders with especially chaotic lifestyles (e.g., drug misusers).

- In two areas, some probation officers thought that the wording of probation orders (since CJA 1991) did not allow them to breach offenders for poor behaviour during probation appointments. This was increasingly dealt with by putting such offenders on 'low grade reporting', where there was no direct contact with the supervising officer.

- For CS orders, there was considerable variation between areas in the allocation of offenders to group, workshop or individual placements. One area had abandoned individual placements because the quality of enforcement by external supervisors had been poor. Another area was less concerned with enforcement issues, and put as many offenders as possible on individual placements, in order to reduce the cost of supervision.

- There was also considerable variation in enforcement practice between different types of order. Probation officers allowed much more leeway both for lateness, and for re-scheduling appointments, than CS officers.

- Probation officers said that they rarely made home visits for enforcement purposes, mainly because of lack of time and concerns about personal safety. However, in the rural districts of two areas, home visits were often used in place of appointments, due to poor transport facilities.

- In one area, probation officers could refer offenders who failed to attend to a specialist follow-up officer. Both the follow-up officer and the referring officers thought that this had improved the speed of enforcement, but monitoring figures were not available to confirm this.

- Three main enforcement issues for combination orders emerged from our study: probation and CS officers felt that magistrates sometimes made combination order disposals for unsuitable offenders, resulting in early recourse to breach action; CS officers generally informed probation officers of any failure to comply on the CS component, but the reverse was seldom true. CS staff in four of the five areas thought that probation officers sometimes allowed too much leeway to offenders who had failed the CS part of the order.

- The contrast between CS and probation order monitoring systems was very noticeable in all areas. CS managers were able to draw on up-to-date information on casefiles from computerised monitoring systems, whereas SPOs relied on retrospective manual casefile sampling and expected probation officers to come to them where there were enforcement problems.

5 Breach action and the court process

Enforcement issues relating to the breach process fall into two main areas: first, breach procedures prior to court appearance; and second, problems and issues occurring at court.

Breach issues prior to court appearance

The time taken from the initiation of breach action to court appearance could vary from three weeks to two months. All 19 Magistrates commented that their confidence in the enforcement of community penalties would improve if this system were speeded up. CS officers also thought the process took too long.

All probation officers agreed that prompt action after a breach was important, although they generally thought that up to four weeks before a court appearance was acceptable. Indeed, six probation officers suggested that the offenders should not appear in court any quicker than this, so that they would have a period of time to assess the offenders' reactions and judge whether to recommend continuation or revocation of the order.

Even when breach cases reached court, further delays were possible. In Area E, the specialist breach officer reported that cases were often adjourned on the first and second hearings, either for the defendant to obtain a solicitor, or for information to be clarified. At the time of the interview (August 1995) the breach officer was aware of 57 such cases for probation and combination orders. Although such figures were not available for the other areas, it seems unlikely that this situation was peculiar to Area E, or to cases where a specialist breach officer was involved.

Three probation officers in Areas A and B, along with all four specialist breach officers in Area B, admitted that poorly completed paperwork by probation officers sometimes contributed to delay in taking a breach case to court. In Area A, two probation officers also admitted that they sometimes delayed a decision to breach purely because of the amount of paperwork involved. CS officers in Area A also complained that while they could issue summonses very quickly for straight CS orders, the involvement of probation officers in combination orders slowed down the process.

At one CS office in Area B, the breach prosecution officer and the magistrates' court were trying out what they referred to as a 'quick breach' system for cases where supervising officers had recommended continuation of an order. This guaranteed an administrative hearing at court within one week of breach action being initiated.[1]

Under this system, the breach prosecution officer sent a letter to offenders requesting that they attend, on a date agreed with the court. The breach prosecution officer also completed the summons paperwork, but did not send this to the magistrates. The breach officer claimed that, in most cases, offenders attended court in response to the letter.[2] If they did not, the completed summons would be sent for signature by the magistrates, and the normal breach process instigated. The community service manager in Area B was in favour of this system, which he considered cheaper and more efficient than ordinary breach arrangements – *"offenders then associate their failure to attend with the court appearance"*.

Failures to comply

All interviewed probation and CS officers commented that failures to comply not related to attendance were sometimes difficult to prove in court – *"You can't send someone home because you suspect they are drunk or on drugs, because you don't have any proof. You have to wait and judge whether they can work properly. You would include information on your suspicions, but it's up to the CS officer and what he decides is good evidence"* (Sessional worker, Area D). In Area B, CS officers also thought that their professional judgement would be questioned if they sent offenders home too often, and as a result, tolerated a certain level of misbehaviour (e.g., use of bad language).

Medical certificates

Medical certificates had caused enforcement problems, particularly for CS orders, in all five areas (see also HMIP report on Automatic Conditional Release: forthcoming). CS officers generally requested a medical certificate within seven days of any absence. Probation officers were not as strict as this, but usually requested medical certificates for absences due to illness or accidents.

---

1   Since these cases were effectively dealt with informally by the courts, this procedure was not employed if revocation or continuation with a fine were being recommended. McWilliams and Murphy (1980: 103-107) also found a similar system operating for breaches of CS in their research.

2   It is important to note that the letter is *not* a summons. An information is laid, but the offender's voluntary appearance at court cures any want of process as a matter of law (see Stones Justices Manual, Paragraph 1-426).

In Areas B and C, CS officers complained that medical certificates were often produced by offenders at the breach hearing, sometimes backdated up to six weeks, and with reasons that one CS officer in Area B described as *"ridiculous....they don't explain why they were absent"*. They commented that the courts nearly always accepted late medical certificates and seemed unwilling to challenge a doctor's judgement. Magistrates agreed that this was usually the case. This could lead to the collapse of some breach cases and, therefore, unnecessary costs.

In Area D, these problems had been resolved by classifying a failure to produce a valid certificate within seven days as a failure to comply.[3] Magistrates accepted this as evidence, as it had been agreed by the Probation Committee.[4] In practice, CS officers gave offenders another appointment solely to produce the certificate -*"If they haven't come before their next working day is due, that would be classed as an unacceptable absence"* (CSO). In fact, CS officers in Areas B and C were keen to see a similar system introduced in their own areas. Area C had already introduced a seven-day limit for the production of medical certificates, but crucially, had not agreed this with the Probation Committee. As a result, courts were still accepting medical certificates at any stage.

Compared to the other areas in this study, CS officers in Area D were more likely to challenge the explanation on a medical certificate as an acceptable excuse, but argued that the courts were less likely to be swayed by this approach. *"If it goes to court, offenders have pleaded not guilty on these. We have more problems with medical certificates than anything else."* (CS Officer, Area D). In direct contrast, the specialist probation breach officer in Area E argued that if an offender arrived at court with a medical certificate that covered the period of a failure to attend *"We'd immediately drop the charge"*.

Generally, all probation and CS officers thought that certificates were a good way of validating explanations of absence. Although medical certificates are not explicitly required under 1995 National Standards, as long as the courts expect them, probation and CS officers said that they would continue to request them. It would therefore seem a matter of good practice to submit a local policy agreement, similar to that of Area D, to Probation Committees.

---

3   Again, McWilliams and Murphy (1980: 105) document these same issues.
4   The same Probation Committee had also agreed not to include travelling time as part of the calculation of hours served on CS orders.

Employers' letters

Employers' letters had caused problems in Areas B, C and D, especially for the enforcement of CS orders. CS officers noted cases where relatives or friends who ran businesses wrote letters covering offenders' absences, without employing them. *"We had one case when a woman had a business, and she used to give all her son's mates letters saying they had to work. Very difficult to prove in court. I had them all in one by one and let them know that I was aware that they were friends of this family and that it was very doubtful about whether they were working from five o'clock in the morning, and not to do it again. It did work, and I was really very lucky that it worked"* (CS Officer, Area D). In these cases, it seemed likely that informal enforcement practices were more effective than breaching and going to court. Both probation and CS officers noted other cases where offenders were forging letters, often using headed notepaper from legitimate businesses. In Area B, if supervising officers suspected letters were not genuine, they referred the case to the specialist breach officers for investigation.

Summonses and warrants

In all five areas, summonses were issued immediately after breach action had been taken. These were sent by first class post, except in Area E, where they were delivered by the follow-up officer. Although there were no available figures, respondents claimed that in most cases, summonses were effective, but if they failed to bring the offender to court, a warrant was issued.

All but three of the 75[5] probation and CS staff interviewed thought that warrants were an ineffective enforcement tool. A typical comment was – *"Warrants are very low priority for the police. I've prosecuted them a year later. The police'll use them for other reasons. If they want to pick someone up they'll go and execute them, otherwise they're low priority"* (SPO, Area D). In addition, both probation and CS officers thought that warrant execution varied considerably between different police stations.

Interviews with police officers in the five areas showed that prioritisation varied according to the type of warrant enforcement system in operation. In Areas A, B and C, warrants were processed by full-time (police) warrants officers and executed by beat officers. Here, as the SPO commented, warrants tended to be prioritised according to their interest to the police for other reasons, for example, to gather intelligence, to make contact with suspects under investigation, to check who was living at an address, etc. By

---

5   This figure excludes sessional workers who had no direct contact with warrants procedure.

contrast, in Areas D and E, warrants were executed by specialist units, and all bench warrants, including community penalties warrants, were given highest priority.

An ACOP[6] survey had drawn attention to the poor execution rate of community penalties warrants by police forces generally, although it should be borne in mind that execution rates alone do not take into account the amount of work put into unsuccessful enquiries by the police. It was unfortunate, therefore, that neither warrant execution rates, nor the number of enquiries made per warrant, were routinely monitored by police officers above the rank of Sergeant. Indeed, there was an indication from the police managers in all areas, and from specialist officers in Areas D and E, that warrants would be given much higher priority if they were made part of a routine management information system, or even of performance indicators. The officers interviewed in the specialist units in Areas D and E also felt that the system by which warrants were executed was more important than whether the police or another agency was responsible.

The specialist officers in Areas D and E had a positive attitude towards community sentences, although they thought that the courts, rather than the probation service, were sometimes too lenient when dealing with breaches. The officers interviewed in Areas A, B and C, with one exception, had a negative attitude towards community penalties, and did not regard them as a serious sentence.

Only two out of the eight magistrates interviewed in Areas A and B were aware of problems with the execution of community penalties warrants. However, the chairman of the CS committee was adamant that – *"Warrants take far too bloody long to be served. This is a really serious complaint I have. You have these coppers walking about the streets bored to tears. Why they can't call on Joe Soap and shove a warrant in his hand I do not understand. I haven't discussed this with a policeman of appropriate rank. I think they are so concerned with their detection record that they see warrants as low priority. They haven't realised that their delays are delays in punishment"*. In Areas D and E, all magistrates thought that the police took too long to execute warrants, and gave them low priority. This was despite the specialist warrants execution systems in both areas.

Court issues

In general, the magistrates interviewed thought they were unlikely to deal with more than eight breach cases a year. However, in Area D, probation and

---

6   Culverhouse (1995).

CS officers normally selected breach dates when the stipendiary magistrate sat, because they had developed a good relationship with him, and thought his decisions were more consistent than those of lay magistrates. While five of the six of the magistrates' courts we contacted in the (five) study areas set aside a day or an afternoon in one court room where magistrates would deal with all breach cases, in most cases 'breach courts' had evolved through probation officers arranging for all breach cases to be heard on particular days, so that they could organise their work accordingly, and there was no attempt, in any area, to select specialist lay magistrates for breach courts.[7] In rural areas, breach courts were not viable because of the small number of breach cases.

Specialist breach officers preferred to use such breach courts, but two non-specialist probation officers complained that there were sometimes breach 'bottlenecks' and that in some cases they had had to list breach cases for other days.

Two probation and three CS officers, mainly in Area B, had observed that breach decisions might vary depending on which magistrates heard the case. All magistrates, including the stipendiary, agreed that this was possible – *"there is no question that offenders receive different community penalty disposals and judgements on breach action depending on the composition of the bench"* (Chairman of Community Penalties Sub-committee, Area A). However, since all magistrates, probation officers and CS officers interviewed thought that concordance rates between breach report recommendations and magistrates' decisions were generally very high, the effects of this inconsistency were likely to be minor. Further, both probation service staff and magistrates confirmed that in the few cases where breach report recommendations were not followed, it was most likely that magistrates would disagree with a recommendation for revocation, and allow the order to continue with a warning, especially where the offender had legal representation – *"I get about 25 to 30% of breaches back again that I don't want back, because magistrates accept that the offender is still willing to work for free in the community"* (CS Officer, Area D).[8]

No CS officers could remember any cases where an order was revoked by magistrates, despite a recommendation for continuation, and magistrates agreed that this was unlikely. However, CS officers, particularly in Areas B and D, complained that even if they successfully applied for breach and revocation, this sometimes achieved very little, since on re-sentencing, the offender might well be given an even longer CS order.

---

7   By chance, it was more likely that some members of the bench would sit more frequently than others on breach court days due to a panel rota system in Area E.
8   See also Broad (1991: 99).

For offenders who were to be returned to an order, all 19 magistrates interviewed said they preferred to add a punitive element to the warning given to offenders regarding future conduct on community orders. For probation orders, they noted this was usually limited to a fine. For CS orders, magistrates occasionally considered awarding further CS hours as a punishment.[9] In most cases, magistrates preferred modest fines consistent with many of the offenders' low incomes. Only two magistrates had considered imposing extra hours, but even here they had looked to probation or CS officers for guidance. One CS officer in Area A thought that this was good practice, as occasionally, magistrates had added extra hours with the result that, in his view, the severity of the sentence was increased out of proportion to the original offence.

Both probation and CS staff stated that *not guilty* pleas for breaches were relatively rare. However, when they did occur, they required more work to prepare and present the case. Offenders pleading *guilty* to breach charges were more likely to have legal representation in Areas D and E, although only probation officers and magistrates in Area E could recall defence solicitors challenging breach evidence in such cases. Interestingly, probation officers in this area said that two firms of solicitors tended to specialise in breach representation. A few breach cases had been lost, for instance, because there was no evidence that offenders had been told when to attend for their next appointments, or even when a warning letter had been received. The specialist breach officer noted that although solicitors only challenged breaches on such technicalities in a few instances, each of these cases required a substantial amount of work to alter subsequent breach practices throughout the service.

There may be an important lesson here. It is likely that breach procedures and evidence are now much more rigorous in Area E than in areas where guilty breach pleas are not challenged. If solicitors elsewhere begin to challenge such breach evidence, it is likely that a significant number of breach cases might be lost, at considerable public expense. Perhaps it would be more cost-effective for probation services to review the adequacy of their procedures in the light of these findings.

A general complaint about Crown Court[10] cases, whether or not they were contested, was that they involved considerably more work and expense, since Probation Service staff had no right of audience in the areas in the study. They were therefore required to employ a solicitor or barrister (in practice usually the county solicitor), brief him/her, and attend court.

---

9   Additional CS orders can be made for both probation and CS orders for up to 60 hours (provided the total for a CS order does not exceed 240 hours) as a result of breach action (see CJA 1991, paras. 2 and 6(3) sch. 2 and s.14) In practice, extra hours were only likely to be considered for CS orders (see Stone, 1994: 34, 36).
10   See Annex IV for the distribution of cases between the two courts in the five study areas.

Magistrates' views on National Standards

Magistrates were asked their views on the impact of NS. Lloyd (1991: 21) foresaw a rise in the number of breaches as a consequence of the introduction of NS for CS orders in 1989. He suggested that, as a result of this, there might be two mutually antagonistic influences on sentencers' confidence in community service disposals: either *"sentencers become irritated by the larger number of breach cases brought before them"*...or the rise in breaches *"could well increase the confidence of sentencers"*.

The 19 magistrates interviewed were unanimous in supporting the second hypothesis. *"There's no dilemma at all, because we see so few cases, and it would have to be phenomenal for clerks to pick it up. We almost always agree with a first breach reports recommendation, because it's been emphasised how, with National Standards, you are brought back quickly, and it's worth giving it another crack if the officer says so, because they know the person"* (Chairman of the bench, Area B).

The magistrates in all five areas did not think it was important for them to know NS breach guidelines, and generally relied solely on the professional judgement of the probation service staff who presented breach cases in court.[11] However, they all thought that the Standards had improved breach presentations considerably. They also preferred to deal with specialist breach officers where possible. These specialists were more familiar with court procedures, and this allowed them to maintain a higher quality of presentation.

Summary

The main findings of this chapter are summarised below.

- Magistrates and CS officers thought that offenders should appear in court as soon as possible after breach action had been initiated. Probation officers agreed that prompt action was important, but preferred some delay (typically around four weeks) so that they could assess the offenders' reactions in deciding whether to recommend revocation or continuation of the order.

- There was some evidence that delays in breach action occurred at court. In particular, adjournments for breach hearings in one area undermined the confidence of the Probation Service staff in the

---

11   HMIP Annual Report 1995, para 1.48, also found that judges and magistrates were often unfamiliar with NS, and Mair et al. (1994: 19) make a similar point.

effectiveness of the breach action and decreased their willingness to initiate such proceedings.

- Probation and CS officers said that in most breach cases summonses were issued, and were usually effective in bringing the offender before the court. If a summons failed, a warrant was issued, although most probation and CS staff had little confidence that they would be executed promptly where warrants were executed by beat officers. Warrants were given much higher priority in the two areas where they were executed by specialist units.

- Most Probation Service staff interviewed favoured specialist breach court arrangements, whereby all newly listed breach cases were heard on a single day. However, specialist courts are not considered suitable in rural areas where there is a low volume of community penalty breach cases.

- Although most supervising officers asked offenders to produce medical certificates within seven days of an absence, the courts tended to accept medical certificates produced much later than this. In one area, this problem had been resolved (for CS orders) with the agreement of the probation committee, by classifying failure to produce a certificate within seven days as a failure to comply.

- Probation and CS staff, along with magistrates, thought that the concordance rate between breach report recommendations and magistrates' decisions was very high. If recommendations were not followed, magistrates were most likely to decide against revocation, in favour of continuation.

- Both probation and CS staff stated that *not guilty* pleas for breaches were relatively rare. Offenders pleading *guilty* to breach charges were more likely to have legal representation in two areas, and in one of these, some notable breach cases had been lost. Although infrequent, such cases required a substantial amount of work to alter subsequent breach practices throughout the service.

- Magistrates were generally not concerned with the details of NS and relied on the officer presenting the breach case for any necessary guidance. They also thought that the quality of breach presentations had improved since the introduction of the Standards.

6 Conclusion

The Government has tried over recent years to encourage the courts to make more effective use of community sentences as a punishment, in addition to the role of such sentences in deterring and rehabilitating offenders. A key part of this approach has involved making community penalties more rigorous, with a clear emphasis on enforcement. This study was commissioned to discover how probation and CS staff ensure compliance, in what circumstances they decide to breach an offender, and how the breach process functions. In this chapter we bring together some of the most important findings and lessons for practice.

Similarities and differences between areas

The pre-National Standards studies reviewed in Chapter 2 found that enforcement was applied unevenly between different probation areas. The results of this first post-National Standards study of enforcement suggest that this is still true.

Local guidelines

Only one of the five areas visited had produced a comprehensive enforcement policy document, covering all aspects of ensuring compliance and the breach process, and for all orders. Generally, local guidelines for dealing with failures to comply on probation were covered in ad hoc memos, issued as problems arose. Guidelines for preparing and prosecuting breach cases were covered in staff handbooks and manuals.

Local CS guidelines were more systematised than those for probation, probably because CS requirements are intrinsically simpler than probation, revolving around turning up for work on time and completing particular pieces of work rather than displaying altered attitudes to offending, or tackling alcohol abuse, and so on. However, CS staff also showed a greater willingness to work to such guidelines; perhaps because their goals were simpler, but it may also reflect the fact that they are drawn from different backgrounds to probation staff and have a different professional ethos.

Non-compliance

In all five areas failures to attend were the most common forms of non-compliance. Breaches for other reasons were more likely on CS orders, and to a lesser extent, on probation orders with requirements. In the latter case, probation officers noted that breach for lack of participation was more likely on requirements run by the Probation Service, for instance, at probation centres, than on requirements run by other agencies, such as drug rehabilitation centres.

Breach

When taking breach action, both probation and CS officers said they most commonly recommended a warning from the court about future conduct, and a continuation of the order. Revocation and re-sentencing were recommended where an order had broken down or where the offender had made no effort to start the order. They were also more likely to recommend revocation if an offender had previously been breached and returned to the order.

While the probation and community service staff largely determine the methods used to ensure compliance, once they begin breach proceedings magistrates and the police also have important roles to play. Clearly, there is little point in the Probation Service reacting swiftly to an offender's persistent non-compliance by instituting breach proceedings if, when an offender fails to answer a summons, the police are slow to enforce the resulting warrant; or the case then takes so long to come to court that the order has been completed.

Probation and CS officers also found it frustrating, when magistrates accepted medical certificates relating to absences which had occurred months before (and which offenders had failed to supply to their supervisors). This both undermined the enforcement process and wasted resources. This problem had been resolved in one of the five areas in relation to CS orders, where failure to produce a medical certificate within seven days was classified as a failure to comply. Crucially, this system was accepted by magistrates because it had been passed by the probation committee. Attempts to operate a similar system in another area, without probation committee involvement, had failed.[1]

---

1   Although medical certificates are not explicitly required under 1995 National Standards, probation and CS officers argued that as long as the courts continue to expect them, they would continue to request them.

Combination Orders

The enforcement of combination orders was considered problematic by most of the probation officers and CS staff interviewed. First, they felt that magistrates sometimes used combination orders for offenders who were incapable of meeting the additional demands these involved, leading inevitably to compliance problems and breach proceedings. Second, while CS officers usually informed probation officers of failures to comply on the CS component, the reverse was seldom true. This was symptomatic of a counterproductive lack of trust: for example, CS staff in four areas thought that probation officers sometimes allowed too much leeway to offenders who had failed the CS part of the order, but who were making satisfactory progress with the probation element. Paradoxically, in the one area where either the CS or probation officer could pursue breach action independently, there were good two-way communications.

Monitoring systems

The contrast between CS and probation order monitoring systems was very noticeable in all areas. CS managers were able to draw on up-to-date information on casefiles from computerised monitoring systems. SPOs relied on retrospective manual casefile sampling and expected probation officers to come to them where there were enforcement problems.

The 'Case Records Administration and Management system' (CRAMS), which is being introduced as part of the National Probation Service Information Systems Strategy (NPSISS), should create a single monitoring system for both CS and probation orders. However, it will be some years before CRAMS is fully operational in all probation services and it is not yet clear whether this system will include all the information currently held on local systems. At least one area is developing its own comprehensive systems and others may follow. Clearly, developments to local systems and CRAMS must be made with an eye to ensuring compatibility.

Training

Another feature common to all five areas was the lack of training carried out on ensuring compliance. Existing training focused on the breach process and preparing for and presenting cases at court. None of the 36 CS officers or sessional workers interviewed had received any formal training in either CS work in general, or in the enforcement process specifically.

National Standards and enforcement practice

It is clear that most probation and CS officers thought that the 1992 National Standards (NS) were helpful in ensuring fair and consistent enforcement practice, and allowed them to use discretion where necessary. However, it was also clear from their replies that probation staff sometimes employed National Standards loosely – for example, recording an attendance when the offender turned up on the same day (or even the next day) rather than at the time specified.

Some probation officers indicated that they would ignore any attempt to reduce their discretion in ways which they considered would interfere with productive work with offenders. For example, changing the accounting period for failures to comply from six to twelve months could be circumvented if officers decide not to record all warning on the offender's file. As monitoring systems in most areas rely on officers bringing problems to their managers' attention or managers inspecting casefiles, such practices would be difficult to detect.

At court, while magistrates generally applauded the introduction of National Standards (crediting them with enhancing the quality of breach case presentations), they saw no need themselves to be familiar with the contents of the Standards or even to act in accordance with them – as they were for the Probation Service, not the courts.

Lessons for practice

In two areas, some probation officers thought that the wording of probation orders (since CJA 1991) did not allow them to breach offenders for poor behaviour during probation appointments. This was increasingly dealt with by putting such offenders on 'low grade reporting', where there was no direct contact with the supervising officer, and which was mainly used for offenders awaiting early revocation for good progress. While some may see this as an efficient way of managing heavy caseloads, as it frees up time to work with better motivated offenders, it is difficult to see it as anything but an abnegation of supervisory responsibilities and as a practice which runs counter to public protection.

Some probation officers dealt with missed appointments by putting the offender on a more frequent reporting cycle. This may be useful in some cases where the non-compliance is wilful but in other cases (as one officer noted) it will simply give offenders twice as many chances to fail.

Appointment cards were used successfully by some probation officers with particular offenders, but it is not clear from this study how useful they would be for the very offenders who are most likely to miss appointments – those with especially chaotic lifestyles (e.g., drug abusers). In these cases, other methods were also employed, such as making appointments coincide with signing-on days for unemployed offenders, or keeping offenders on fortnightly reporting at the same time and day of the week for the duration of an order.

In one area, on a first failure to attend, probation officers could refer offenders for a visit by a 'follow-up' officer. This officer reported any explanations given by the offender to the supervising officer and tried to trace offenders who had moved address without having notified the probation service. Although no hard evidence was available, probation officers and the follow up officer considered this to be a more effective way of ensuring compliance than sending warning letters by post.

Special breach courts were held in four of the five areas in this study. They were set up for administrative convenience – so that cases could be listed to a particular day, rather than arranging each hearing separately. Of course, specialist courts may not be viable in (mainly rural) areas where the number of breaches is small. Overall, it is clear that methods for ensuring compliance and breaching offenders varied not only between areas but between teams and officers. This lack of system may result in pockets of very poor practice, but it has also facilitated some enterprising and innovative approaches to encouraging compliance and dealing with breach.

Annex I: Background information and sample details

Area A

Probation service staff interviewed: 17. One assistant chief probation officer (ACPO); three senior probation officers; six probation officers; one senior community service officer (SCSO); three CS officers; and three CS sessional supervisors.

Interviews were carried out at one police station with the following personnel: the Criminal Justice Office manager (Chief Inspector); Detective Chief Inspector: two Warrants Officers (constables); a local intelligence officer (LIO) and a beat or sector officer (constable).

Magistrates interviewed: one PSD chairman of the bench; one chairman of the probation committee; one chairman of the community penalties sub-committee; and an ordinary magistrate.

Area B

Probation service staff interviewed: 18. Two ACPOs; three SPOs; four probation officers; the community service manager; three CS officers; one CS full-time supervisor; one CS sessional supervisor; and three breach prosecution officers.

Interviews were carried out at one police station with the following personnel: the station operations manager (Chief Inspector); the Custody Inspector; a Section Sergeant; the Warrants Officer (constable); and a Beat Constable.

Magistrates interviewed: one PSD chairman of the bench; one vice-chairman of the probation committee; one chairman of the probation liaison committee; and an ordinary magistrate.

Area C

Interviews were carried out with 20 staff: two ACPOs; five SPOs (covering field probation and CS); four probation officers (from probation and CS);

57

three CS officers; three specialist court/breach officers; and three CS sessional supervisors (covering group projects, workshops and individual placements).

Interviews were carried out at one police station with the following personnel: the Criminal Justice Office manager (Chief Inspector); Detective Chief Inspector: one Sergeant (Criminal Justice Officer, two Warrants Officers (one police, one civilian); and a beat or sector sergeant.

Magistrates interviewed: one PSD chairman of the bench; one stipendiary magistrate; and one member of the probation liaison committee.

Area D

Probation service staff interviewed: 16. One ACPO (community sentences policy); three SPOs; four probation officers; one specialist breach (probation) officer; one CS manager; two CS officers; one CS project organiser; one full-time CS supervisor; and two CS sessional supervisors.

Interviews were carried out in one warrants office with: the Chief Inspector (Operations Manager); one police warrants officer (constable); one civilian warrants officer; and, a civilian computer operator.

Magistrates interviewed: one stipendiary magistrate; one PSD chairman of the bench; one joint vice-chairman of both probation committee and probation liaison committee; and, one ordinary magistrate.

Area E

Probation service staff interviewed: 18. One ACPO (CS); four SPOs (including the CS manager); four probation officers (including CS probation officer); one specialist probation breach officer; five CS officers; two sessional supervisors and the follow up officer (PSO).

Interviews were carried out at one police station with: one Chief Superintendent (Divisional Commander); one Superintendent (Operations); two Chief Inspectors (Administration of Justice Unit and Section Commander); one section Sergeant; two constables (beat officers); one local intelligence officer; one warrants office manager (civilian); and one warrants officer (civilian).

Magistrates interviewed: one PSD chairman of the bench; one chairman of probation liaison committee; one member of probation committee; and, one ordinary magistrate.

Annex II: The enforcement process and National Standards

National Standards are central to the enforcement of community penalties, and provide a clear outline of minimum requirements. This annex provides a summary of the enforcement content of the Standards which were in force at the time this research was carried out, and notes where the current Standards differ.

Summary of National Standards and enforcement

National Standards were introduced for CS orders in 1989 and extended to all community sentences, except Attendance Centre orders, in October 1992. These standards stipulated that to enforce orders effectively, the Probation Service should ensure an offender's consent to, and compliance with an order, but take appropriate action where this could not be achieved (Home Office 1992: 39, 75). However, the Standards acknowledged that how and when to take enforcement action were matters for the individual practitioners and services (ibid., 4), although any decision to delay breach action, *"in limited circumstances only"*, required the agreement of a Senior Probation Officer (or equivalent); and all instances of failure to comply, decisions made, and action taken, were to be noted on case records (ibid.: 40, 76). The 1995 Standards also leave similar room for departure from NS *"in exceptional circumstances"* (Home Office 1995c, 1). In addition Chief Probation Officers were (and are) also required to establish 'local practice guidance' on the application of NS for, among other things, the handling of enforcement and breach proceedings (Home Office, 1992: 42, 77 and 1995c, 3).

Enforcement guidelines in the 1992 NS were largely the same for probation, CS and combination orders. Any apparent failure to comply with the requirements of an order (e.g. lateness, failure to attend, unacceptable performance/behaviour, etc.) had to be followed up promptly, *"normally within two working days"* (Home Office, 1992: 39, 75). The supervising officer had to seek an explanation from the offender and decide whether it was acceptable. If the explanation was unacceptable, a failure to comply had to be recorded, and the offender warned, verbally in the first instance, and in writing on subsequent occasions, of the likely consequences of continued failure to comply (ibid.: 39, 76). Under the new Standards, all warnings must be in writing (Home Office, 1995c: 22, 39). The 1992 NS also provided for personal circumstances to be taken into account in establishing the level of premeditation for failures to comply (ibid.: 39, 76), but the current Standards make no reference to this.

The 1992 Standards stated that breach action might be appropriate immediately depending on the nature of the failure to comply. In other cases *"breach action should be taken after no more than three instances of failure to comply with the order"* (ibid.: 40, 76), within a six-month period (twelve months under 1995 NS).

Offenders on CS were normally expected to continue working once breach action was pending on a CS order, and good or bad conduct during this period could be taken into account at a breach hearing. Any further failure to comply would normally result in the offender being suspended from the order until after the breach hearing (ibid., 77), although this point is not made explicit in the 1995 Standards (see Home Office, 1995c, 39).

For combination orders, the 1992 Standards stated that a maximum of three failures to comply on either the probation, or the CS element of an order, should result in breach action. There was provision to consider an offender's overall performance in borderline cases, but this is not mentioned in the 1995 Standards (Home Office 1992, 84 cf. 1995c, 42). The 1992 Standards also stipulated that a probation officer should be given overall responsibility for supervising the order (ibid., 82), whereas the 1995 Standards allow this overall responsibility to be taken by either the probation or CS officer (Home Office 1995c, 41). Both 1992 and 1995 Standards also add that probation and CS supervisors on combination orders should always liaise prior to the commencement of breach proceedings (Home Office 1992, 83 and 1995c, 41).

Finally, the 1992 Standards declared that the Probation Service had an important role in both proving breach and in advising a court whether to allow the order to continue with a warning about future action conduct, or to revoke the order and re-sentence the offender.

Annex III: Community sentence breach data

Figures for England and Wales are used in these tables,[1] but it is not possible to provide the equivalent data for each of the five areas in the study, since they are collected by police force area. The term 'breach ratio' is employed, as opposed to 'breach rate', since breaches which occurred in 1994 may relate to orders which commenced in earlier years, and because the data cannot show how often multiple breaches occurred on single orders.

Table 1:
Community sentences and breaches in England and Wales: 1994[2]

Type of order	No. of orders imposed	No. of breaches	Breach ratio
Probation	50,535	4,665	9.2%
CS	49,469	11,680	23.6%
Combination	12,399	2,777	22.4%

1   Based on a further breakdown of Tables 7.11 and 7.22 of Criminal Statistics 1994.
2   Breach cases that were combined with a hearing for a further offence are included in this table.

Table 2:
Estimated proportion of breaches resulting in revocation, continuation and discharge, in England and Wales: 1994[3]

Type of order	Breach and revocation[4]	Breach and continuation[5]	Breach and discharge[6]
Probation	59%	33%	7%
CS	44%	51%	5%
Combination	73%	25%	2%

---

3   In order to arrive at the headings presented in the table, we have had to use the findings produced by this study to interpret a number of different outcomes resulting from breach cases. The assumptions made are presented in the following footnotes. However, it is worth noting first that breaches where no action is taken, i.e. the offender receives a 'warning' about future conduct on the order, but is not awarded a fine and/or extra hours, are not returned to the Home Office, and there may be some under-counting of breaches due to this. Figures available for CS orders in Area B suggest that 13 per cent of breaches are of this type, but it is not known whether this varies depending on the type of community order. Where the row percentages in Table 2 do not add up to 100 per cent, this is due to the omission of the 'otherwise dealt with' category. This is made up of very small individual categories such as data errors, restriction and hospital orders (Mental Health Act 1983), etc. Breach cases that were combined with a hearing for a further offence were *not* included in this table.

4   This category has been estimated by combining the number of breach outcomes resulting in immediate custody, 'further community sentences' and fully suspended sentences. The majority of these cases are likely to have been breaches resulting in revocation and resentencing. (Where breach cases were combined with a hearing for a further offence, they have been excluded from the table.) For CS orders, magistrates sometimes make a short additional CS order as a penalty for breach of an existing CS order, although interviews with magistrates in the enforcement study suggested that this was relatively rare.

5   The majority of fines are likely to be the result of breaches of an order where continuation has been recommended and/or granted.

6   These represent a small but significant category of breach outcomes. Two magistrates in the enforcement study hinted at their possible importance. It is likely these discharges are for breaches which have been recommended for revocation near the end of an order, where supervising officers and/or magistrates do not think it is worth imposing a further penalty.

Annex IV: Offenders sentenced to community penalties in magistrates' courts as a proportion of offenders sentenced to community penalties in all courts: 1993[1]

	Probation order	CS order	Combination order
Area A	76%	68%	74%
Area B	76%	66%	75%
Area C	70%	69%	59%
Area D	76%	71%	81%
Area E	81%	79%	62%

1   Unpublished figures supplied by HO Statistics Division, March 1995.

References

Audit Commission (1991) *Going straight: developing good practice in the probation service.* London: HMSO.

Broad, B. (1991) *Punishment Under Pressure: The Probation Service in the Inner City.* Kingsley: London.

Brockington, N. and Shaw, M. (1986) *Tracking the trackers.* RPU Bulletin 22.

Burnett, R. (1996) *Fitting supervision to offenders: assessment and allocation decisions in the Probation Service.* Home Office Research Study No.153. London: HMSO.

Chandler, D. (1987) *Fine Enforcement: ideas from a survey. Institute of Criminology* Occasional Paper No.15. University of Cambridge.

Craig, Y. (1979) *Supervision: Casework, Counselling, Companionship, Control.* Probation Journal, Vol.23, No.3 1976.

Culverhouse, L. J. (1995). *Response to questionnaire relating to outstanding warrants and enforcement,* ACPO internal document.

Davies, M. (1969) *Probationers in their Social Environment.* Home Office Research Study No.2. London: HMSO.

Davies, M. (1970) *Financial Penalties and Probation.* Home Office Research Study No.5. London: HMSO.

Davies, M. (1979) *Through the eyes of the probationer.* Probation Journal, 26, 3 pp.84-88.

Davies, M. (1984) *Community-based alternatives to custody: the right place for the probation service.* Prison Journal 53 (new series), 2-5.

Davies, G., Boswell, G. and Wright, A. (1989) *Skills, knowledge and qualities in probation practice* (4 vols). Norwich: Probation Monographs, University of East Anglia.

Drakeford, M. (1993) *The Probation Service, Breach and the Criminal Justice Act 1991.* The Howard Journal, Vol.32, No.4, November 1993.

Dunlop, A. B. (1980) *Junior Attendance Centres.* Home Office Research Study No.60. London: HMSO.

Eysenck, S. (1986) *Justice of the Peace,* Vol.150, pp.808-809.

Francis, J. (1993) *Combination Confusion.* Community Care, 15 July 1993, pp12-13.

Gelsthorpe, L. and Morris, A. (1983) *Attendance Centres: Policy and Practice.* The Howard Journal, Vol.22, No.2.

Giller, H. and Morris, A. (1978), *Supervision orders: the routinization of treatment.* The Howard Journal, Vol.17, No.3.

Graham, V. (1995). *Phoenix rises.* Police Review, 2 June 1995.

Harris, R. (1980) *A changing service: the case for separating 'care' and 'control' in probation practice.* British Journal of Social Work, 10, 2, pp. 163-184.

Harris, R. and Webb, D. (1983) *Social work and the supervision order.* RPU Bulletin, No.16.

Heritage, B. (1993) *Thresholds and Proportionality: What difference?* Probation Bulletin, 40, 1, March 1993, pp30-31.

Hoggarth, E. A. (1991) *Selection for community service orders.* Aldershot: Avebury.

HM Inspectorate of Probation (1993) *HM Inspectorate of Probation Annual Report,* 1992-93.

HM Inspectorate of Probation (1995a) *Community Service.* Report of a Thematic Inspection, 1994. London: HMIP.

HM Inspectorate of Probation (1995b) *Dealing with Dangerous People: The Probation Service and Public Protection.* Report of a Thematic Inspection, 1995. London: HMIP.

HM Inspectorate of Probation (1996a) *Probation Orders with Additional Requirements.* Report of a Thematic Inspection, 1995. London: HMIP.

HM Inspectorate of Probation (1996b) *HM Inspectorate of Probation Annual Report, 1995.*

HM Inspectorate of Probation (1996c) *An enquiry into breach and prosecution of Automatic Conditional Release Licences.* Unpublished HMIP report.

Home Office (1974) *Community Service by offenders:* HO Circular HOC 197/1974, plus accompanying 'Memorandum of Guidance'.

Home Office (1982) *Report on the Working Group on Magistrates' Courts.* London: Home Office.

Home Office (1988) *Punishment, Custody and the Community.* London: HMSO.

Home Office Circular (1989) No.18.

Home Office (1990a) *Crime, Justice and Protecting the public,* Cm. 965.

Home Office (1990b) *Supervision and punishment in the community,* Cm. 966.

Home Office (1992) *National standards for the supervision of offenders in the community.* London: Home Office, Department of Health and Welsh Office.

Home Office (1993) *The Criminal Justice Act Inspection 1991.* London: HMSO.

Home Office (1994) *The Probation Service: Three Year Plan for the Probation Service 1994-1997.* London: HMSO 1/94.

Home Office, (1995a) *Review of police core and ancillary tasks.* London: HMSO.

Home Office, (1995b) *Criminal Statistics: England and Wales 1994.* London: HMSO.

Home Office (1995c) *National standards for the supervision of offenders in the community.* London: Home Office, Department of Health and Welsh Office.

Home Office, (1996) *Probation Statistics: England and Wales 1994.* London: Home Office.

Humphrey, C. and Pease, K. (1992) *Effectiveness Measurement in Probation: A View from the Troops.* The Howard Journal Vol.31, No.1, February 1992.

James, A. (1979) *Sentenced to Surveillance?* Probation Journal, Vol.26, No.1, 1979.

Lawson, C. (1978) *The Probation Officer as prosecutor: a study of proceedings for breach of requirements in probation.* Cambridge: Institute of Criminology.

Lewis, H. and Mair, G. (1988) *Bail and Probation work II: the use of London probation/bail hostels for bailees.* Research and Planning Unit Paper 50. London: HMSO.

Lloyd, C. (1991) *National Standards for Community Service Orders: the first two years of operation.* RPU Bulletin 31.

Lloyd, P. M. (1994) *What is the place of combination orders at magistrates' courts?* Justice of the Peace, 158, 10, March 5 1994, 149-150.

Mair, G. (1984) *The senior attendance centre as an alternative to custody.* RPU Bulletin No. 18.

Mair, G. (1987) *Senior attendance centres and day centres.* RPU Bulletin 23. London: HMSO.

Mair, G. (1988) *Probation Day Centres.* Home Office Research Study No.100. London: HMSO.

Mair, G. (1991) *Part Time Punishment? The Origins and Development of Senior Attendance Centres.* London: HMSO.

Mair, G. and Lloyd, C. (1989) *Money Payment Supervision Orders: Probation policy and practice.* Home Office Research Study No.114. London: HMSO.

Mair, G., Sibbitt, R. and Crisp, D. (1994) *The Combination Order – An Interim Report.* Home Office Research and Planning Unit (unpublished).

Marshall, G. (1978) *Controlling Care.* Probation Journal, Vol.25, No.1 1978.

May, C. (1995) *Measuring the Satisfaction of Courts with the Probation Service.* Home Office Research Study No.144. London: HMSO.

McIvor, G. (1990) *Community Service and Custody in Scotland.* The Howard Journal Vol.29, No.2, May 1990.

McIvor, G. (1991) *Community Service Work Placements.* The Howard Journal Vol.30, No.1, February 1991.

McWilliams, W. (1989) *Community service national standards: practice and sentencing.* Probation Journal, 36, 121-6.

McWilliams, W. and Murphy, N. (1980) *'Breach of Community Service Orders'* in Pease K. and McWilliams, W. (Eds.) *Community Service by Order.* Edinburgh: Scottish Academic Press.

McWilliams, W. and Pease K. (1990) *Probation Practice and an End to Punishment.* The Howard Journal, Vol.29, No.1, February 1990.

Moloney, N. (1995) *Combination orders: their history, use and impact.* Social Work Monograph No. 137. Norwich: University of East Anglia.

Moore, T. G. and Wilkinson, T. P. (1994) *Youth Court: A guide to the Law and Practice.* Longman: London.

Mott, J. (1985) *Punishment practice by prison Boards of Visitors.* RPU Bulletin No. 19.

Moxon, D. (1983) *Fine default: unemployment and the use of imprisonment.* RPU Bulletin No.16.

Moxon, D. (1991) *Developments in fines and fine enforcement.* RPU Bulletin 30.

Moxon, D., Sutton, M. and Hedderman, C. (1990) *Unit Fines: experiments in four courts.* Research and Planning Unit Paper No.59. London: HMSO.

Moxon, D., Corkery, J. M. and Hedderman, C. (1992) *Developments in the use of compensation orders in Magistrates' Courts since October 1988.* Home Office Research Study No.126. London HMSO.

Moxon, D. (1993) *Use of compensation orders in Magistrates' Courts.* RPU Bulletin 33.

National Association for the Care and Resettlement of Offenders (1981) *Fine Default: Report of a NACRO Working Party.* London: HMSO.

Newburn, T. with the assistance of de Peyrecave, H. (1988) *The use and enforcement of compensation orders in Magistrates' Courts.* Home Office Research Study No.102. London: HMSO.

Nuttall, C. P. with Barnard, E. E., Fowles, A. J., Frost, A., Hammond, P., Mayhew, P., Pease, K., Tarling, R. and Weatheritt, M. J., (1977) *Parole in England and Wales* Home Office Research Unit Report No.38. London: HMSO.

North Wales Probation Service (1994) *Internal inspection of Crown Court Work* (August 1994).

Palmer, S. (1979) *Style and Regime in Probation Hostels.* Probation Journal, Vol.26, No.3, 1979.

Pease, K. (1985) *'Community Service Orders'* in Tonry, M. and Morris, N. (Eds.) *Crime and Justice: An Annual Review of Research,* Vol.6. Chicago: University of Chicago Press.

Pease, K., Billingham, S. and Earnshaw, I. (1977) *Community Service Assessed in 1976.* Home Office Research Study No.39. London:HMSO.

Pease, K., Durkin, P., Earnshaw, I., Payne, D. And Thorpe J. (1975) *Community Service Orders.* Home Office Research Study No. 29. London: HMSO.

Pease, K. and West J. (1977) *Community Service Orders: the way ahead.* RPU Bulletin No.4.

Read, G. (1980) *'Area differences in community service operation'* in Pease K. and McWilliams, W. (Eds.) *Community Service by Order.* Edinburgh: Scottish Academic Press.

Sheppard, B. (1980) *Research into aspects of probation.* RPU Bulletin No.10.

Simon, F. And Wilson, S. (1975) *Field Wing Bail Hostel: The First Nine Months.* Home Office Research Study No.30. London: HMSO.

Sinclair, I. (1971) *Hostels for Probationers.* Home Office Research Study No.6. London: HMSO.

Sinclair, I. and Clarke, R. V. G. (1973) *Acting-out and its significance for the residential treatment of delinquents.* Journal of Child Psychology and Psychiatry, 14, pp.283-291.

Skinns, C. D. (1990) *Community service practice.* British Journal of Criminology, 30, Winter 1990, pp.65-80.

Softley, P. (1973) *A Survey of Fine Enforcement.* Home Office Research Study No.16. London: HMSO.

Softley, P. (1978) *Fines in Magistrates' Courts.* Home Office Research Study No.46. London: HMSO.

Softley, P. and Moxon, D. (1982) *Fine Enforcement.* Research and Planning Unit Paper 12, London: HMSO.

Stone, N. (1994) *A companion guide to enforcement.* Owen Wells: Ilkley.

Stone, N. (1995) *Revocation and resentence following breach of a community sentence.* The Magistrate, June 1995, pp. 106-107.

Teasdale, T. (1989) *Management Information System for the Magistrates' Courts: performance indicators for fine enforcement.* RPU Bulletin 27.

Vass, A. A. (1980a) *Law Enforcement in Community Service: Probation, Defence or Prosecution?* Probation Journal, Vol.27, No.4, 1980.

Vass, A. A. (1980b) *Law Enforcement in Community Service,* in Harding, J. (Ed.) *Probation and the Community,* 83-99. London: Tavistock Publications.

Vass, A. A. (1981) *Community Service for Juveniles? A Critical Comment.* Probation Journal, 28: 44-9.

Vass, A. A. (1982) *The Enforcement of Community Service Orders in One Area of Southern England.* PhD thesis, University of London.

Vass, A. A. (1983) *A Working Sketch of a Community Service Session.* Probation Journal, 30:148-52.

Vass, A. A. (1984a) *Sentenced to Labour: close encounters with a prison substitute.* St Ives: Venus Academica.

Vass, A. A. (1984b) *Breach of Community Service Orders and the Application of Sanctions.* Occasional Paper No.12, Faculty of Social Science, Middlesex Polytechnic.

Vass, A. A. (1986) *Community Service: Areas of Concern and Suggestions for Change.* Howard Journal, Vol.25, No.2, pp. 100-111.

Vass, A. A. (1988a) *The Future of Community Service and the Role of the Ancillary.* Community Service Newsletter, 24:3-10.

Vass, A. A. (1988b) *The Marginality of Community Service and the Threat of Privatisation.* Probation Journal, 35/2:48-51.

Vass, A. A. (1989) *The Community Service Order as a Public and Private Enterprise.* British Journal of Criminology, Vol.29, No.3 Summer 1989.

Vass, A. A. (1990) *Alternatives to Prison: punishment, custody and the community.* London: Sage.

Vass, A. A. and Weston, A. (1990) *Probation day centres as an alternative to custody: a 'Trojan Horse' examined.* British Journal of Criminology, Vol.30, No.2 Spring 1990.

Ward, R. and Ward, S. (1993) *Community Sentences: Law and Practice.* London: Blackstone.

West Midlands Probation Service/ACOP (1994) *The same day report: expedited justice?,* June 1994, West Midlands Probation Service.

Wilkinson, C. (1990) *Community Service Orders: Monitoring National Standards.* University of Birmingham Department of Social Policy and Social Work.

Willis, A. (1981) *Social welfare and social control: a survey of young men on probation.* RPU Bulletin 8.

Young, W. (1979) *Community Service Orders: The Development and Use of a New Penal Measure.* London: Heinemann.

Publications

List of research publications

A list of research reports for the last three years is provided below. A **full** list of publications is available on request from the Research and Statistics Directorate Information and Publications Group.

Home Office Research Studies (HORS)

130. **Car theft: the offender's perspective.** Roy Light, Claire Nee and Helen Ingham. 1993. x + 89pp. (0 11 341069 7).

131. **Housing, Community and Crime: The Impact of the Priority Estates Project.** Janet Foster and Timothy Hope with assistance from Lizanne Dowds and Mike Sutton. 1993. xi + 118pp. (0 11 341078 6).

132. **The 1992 British Crime Survey.** Pat Mayhew, Natalie Aye Maung and Catriona Mirrlees-Black. 1993. xiii + 206pp. (0 11 341094 8).

133. **Intensive Probation in England and Wales: an evaluation.** George Mair, Charles Lloyd, Claire Nee and Rae Sibbett. 1994. xiv + 143pp. (0 11 341114 6).

134. **Contacts between Police and Public: findings from the 1992 British Crime Survey.** Wesley G Skogan. 1995. ix + 93pp. (0 11 341115 4).

135. **Policing low-level disorder: Police use of Section 5 of the Public Order Act 1986.** David Brown and Tom Ellis. 1994. ix + 69pp. (0 11 341116 2).

136. **Explaining reconviction rates: A critical analysis.** Charles Lloyd, George Mair and Mike Hough. 1995. xiv + 103pp. (0 11 341117 0).

137. **Case Screening by the Crown Prosecution Service: How and why cases are terminated.** Debbie Crisp and David Moxon. 1995. viii + 66pp. (0 11 341137 5).

138. **Public Interest Case Assessment Schemes.** Debbie Crisp, Claire Whittaker and Jessica Harris. 1995. x + 58pp. (0 11 341139 1).

139. **Policing domestic violence in the 1990s.** Sharon Grace. 1995. x + 74pp. (0 11 341140 5).

140. **Young people, victimisation and the police: British Crime Survey findings on experiences and attitudes of 12 to 15 year olds.** Natalie Aye Maung. 1995. xii + 140pp. (0 11 341150 2).

141. **The Settlement of refugees in Britain.** Jenny Carey-Wood, Karen Duke, Valerie Karn and Tony Marshall. 1995. xii + 133pp. (0 11 341145 6).

142. **Vietnamese Refugees since 1982.** Karen Duke and Tony Marshall. 1995. x + 62pp. (0 11 341147 2).

143. **The Parish Special Constables Scheme.** Peter Southgate, Tom Bucke and Carole Byron. 1995. x + 59pp. (1 85893 458 3).

144. **Measuring the Satisfaction of the Courts with the Probation Service.** Chris May. 1995. x + 76pp. (1 85893 483 4).

145. **Young people and crime.** John Graham and Benjamin Bowling. 1995. xv + 142pp. (1 85893 551 2).

146. **Crime against retail and manufacturing premises: findings from the 1994 Commercial Victimisation Survey.** Catriona Mirrlees-Black and Alec Ross. 1995. xi + 110pp. (1 85893 554 7).

147. **Anxiety about crime: findings from the 1994 British Crime Survey.** Michael Hough. 1995. viii + 92pp. (1 85893 553 9).

148. **The ILPS Methadone Prescribing Project.** Rae Sibbitt. 1996. viii + 69pp. (1 85893 485 0).

149. **To scare straight or educate? The British experience of day visits to prison for young people.** Charles Lloyd. 1996. xi + 60pp. (1 85893 570 9).

150. **Predicting reoffending for Discretionary Conditional Release.** John B Copas, Peter Marshall and Roger Tarling. 1996. vii + 49pp. (1 85893 576 8).

151. **Drug misuse declared: results of the 1994 British Crime Survey.** Malcom Ramsay and Andrew Percy. 1996. xv + 131pp. (1 85893 628 4).

152. **An Evaluation of the Introduction and Operation of the Youth Court.** David O'Mahony and Kevin Haines. 1996. viii + 70pp. (1 85893 579 2).

153. **Fitting supervision to offenders: assessment and allocation decisions in the Probation Service.** Ros Burnett. 1996. xi + 99pp. (1 85893 599 7).

156. **Automatic Conditional Release: the first two years.** Mike Maguire, Brigitte Perroud and Peter Raynor. 1996. x + 114pp. (1 85893 659 4).

157. **Testing obscenity: an international comparison of laws and controls relating to obscene material.** Sharon Grace. 1996. ix + 46pp. (1 85893 672 1).

Nos 154 and 155 not published yet.

Research and Planning Unit Papers (RPUP)

72. **The National Probation Survey 1990.** Chris May. 1993.

73. **Public satisfaction with police services.** Peter Southgate and Debbie Crisp. 1993.

74. **Disqualification from driving: an effective penalty?** Catriona Mirrlees-Black. 1993.

75. **Detention under the Prevention of Terrorism (Temporary Provisions) Act 1989: Access to legal advice and outside contact.** David Brown. 1993.

76. **Panel assessment schemes for mentally disordered offenders.** Carol Hedderman. 1993.

77. **Cash-limiting the probation service: a case study in resource allocation.** Simon Field and Mike Hough. 1993.

78. **The probation response to drug misuse.** Claire Nee and Rae Sibbitt. 1993.

79   **Approval of rifle and target shooting clubs: the effects of the new and revised criteria.** John Martin Corkery. 1993.

80.   **The long-term needs of victims: a review of the literature.** Tim Newburn. 1993.

81.   **The welfare needs of unconvicted prisoners.** Diane Caddle and Sheila White. 1994.

82.   **Racially motivated crime: a British Crime Survey analysis.** Natalie Aye Maung and Catriona Mirrlees-Black. 1994.

83.   **Mathematical models for forecasting Passport demand.** Andy Jones and John MacLeod. 1994.

84.   **The theft of firearms**. John Corkery. 1994.

85.   **Equal opportunities and the Fire Service.** Tom Bucke. 1994.

86.   **Drug Education Amongst Teenagers: a 1992 British Crime Survey Analysis**. Lizanne Dowds and Judith Redfern. 1995.

87.   **Group 4 Prisoner Escort Service: a survey of customer satisfaction.** Claire Nee. 1994.

88.   **Special Considerations: Issues for the Management and Organisation of the Volunteer Police.** Catriona Mirrlees-Black and Carole Byron. 1995.

89.   **Self-reported drug misuse in England and Wales: findings from the 1992 British Crime Survey.** Joy Mott and Catriona Mirrlees-Black. 1995.

90.   **Improving bail decisions: the bail process project, phase 1.** John Burrows, Paul Henderson and Patricia Morgan. 1995.

91.   **Practitioners' views of the Criminal Justice Act: a survey of criminal justice agencies.** George Mair and Chris May. 1995.

92.   **Obscene, threatening and other troublesome telephone calls to women in England and Wales: 1982-1992.** Wendy Buck, Michael Chatterton and Ken Pease. 1995.

93.   **A survey of the prisoner escort and custody service provided by Group 4 and by Securicor Custodial Services.** Diane Caddle. 1995.

Research Findings

1. **Magistrates' court or Crown Court? Mode of trial decisions and their impact on sentencing.** Carol Hedderman and David Moxon. 1992.

2. **Surveying crime: findings from the 1992 British Crime Survey.** Pat Mayhew and Natalie Aye Maung. 1992. (Out of print).

3. **Car Theft: the offenders' perspective.** Claire Nee. 1993.

4. **The National Prison Survey 1991: main findings.** Roy Walmsley, Liz Howard and Sheila White. 1993.

5. **Changing the Code: Police detention under the revised PACE codes of practice.** David Brown, Tom Ellis and Karen Larcombe. 1993.

6. **Rifle and pistol target shooting clubs: The effects of new approval criteria.** John M. Corkery. 1993.

7. **Self-reported drug misuse in England and Wales. Main findings from the 1992 British Crime Survey.** Joy Mott and Catriona Mirrlees-Black. 1993.

8. **Findings from the International Crime Survey.** Pat Mayhew. 1994.

9. **Fear of Crime: Findings from the 1992 British Crime Survey.** Catriona Mirrlees-Black and Natalie Aye Maung. 1994.

10. **Does the Criminal Justice system treat men and women differently?** Carol Hedderman and Mike Hough. 1994.

11. **Participation in Neighbourhood Watch: Findings from the 1992 British Crime Survey.** Lizanne Dowds and Pat Mayhew. 1994.

12. **Explaining Reconviction Rates: A Critical Analysis.** Charles Lloyd, George Mair and Mike Hough. 1995.

13. **Equal opportunities and the Fire Service.** Tom Bucke. 1994.

14. **Trends in Crime: Findings from the 1994 British Crime Survey.** Pat Mayhew, Catriona Mirrlees-Black and Natalie Aye Maung. 1994.

15. **Intensive Probation in England and Wales: an evaluation**. George Mair, Charles Lloyd, Claire Nee and Rae Sibbitt. 1995.

16. **The settlement of refugees in Britain**. Jenny Carey-Wood, Karen Duke, Valerie Karn and Tony Marshall. 1995.

17. **Young people, victimisation and the police: British Crime Survey findings on experiences and attitudes of 12- to 15- year-olds.** Natalie Aye Maung.

18. **Vietnamese Refugees since 1982.** Karen Duke and Tony Marshall. 1995.

19. **Supervision of Restricted Patients in the Community.** Suzanne Dell and Adrian Grounds. 1995.

20. **Videotaping children's evidence: an evaluation.** Graham Davies, Clare Wilson, Rebecca Mitchell and John Milsom. 1995.

21. **The mentally disordered and the police.** Graham Robertson, Richard Pearson and Robert Gibb. 1995.

22. **Preparing records of taped interviews.** Andrew Hooke and Jim Knox. 1995.

23. **Obscene, threatening and other troublesome telephone calls to women: Findings from the British Crime Survey.** Wendy Buck, Michael Chatterton and Ken Pease. 1995.

24. **Young people and crime.** John Graham and Ben Bowling. 1995.

25. **Anxiety about crime: Findings from the 1994 British Crime Survey.** Michael Hough. 1995.

26. **Crime against retail premises in 1993.** Catriona Mirrlees-Black and Alec Ross. 1995.

27. **Crime against manufacturing premises in 1993.** Catriona Mirrlees-Black and Alec Ross. 1995.

28. **Policing and the public: findings from the 1994 British Crime Survey.** Tom Bucke. 1995.

29. **The Child Witness Pack – An Evaluation.** Joyce Plotnikoff and Richard Woolfson. 1995.

30.	**To scare straight or educate? The British experience of day visits to prison for young people.** Charles Lloyd. 1996.

31.	**The ADT drug treatment programme at HMP Downview – a preliminary evaluation.** Elaine Player and Carol Martin. 1996.

32.	**Wolds remand prison – an evaluation.** Keith Bottomley, Adrian James, Emma Clare and Alison Liebling. 1996.

33.	**Drug misuse declared: results of the 1994 British Crime Survey.** Malcolm Ramsay and Andrew Percy. 1996.

34.	**Crack cocaine and drugs-crime careers.** Howard Parker and Tim Bottomley. 1996.

35.	**Imprisonment for fine default.** David Moxon and Claire Whittaker. 1996.

36.	**Fine impositions and enforcement following the Criminal Justice Act 1993.** Elizabeth Charman, Bryan Gibson, Terry Honess and Rod Morgan. 1996.

Research Bulletin

The Research Bulletin is published twice each year and contains short articles on recent research.

Occasional Papers

Employment opportunities for offenders. David Downes. 1993.

Sex offenders: a framework for the evaluation of community-based treatment. Mary Barker and Rod Morgan. 1993.

Suicide attempts and self-injury in male prisons. Alison Liebling and Helen Krarup. 1993.

Measurement of caseload weightings associated with the Children Act. Richard J. Gadsden and Graham J. Worsdale. 1994. (Available from the RSD Information and Publications Group).

Managing difficult prisoners: The Lincoln and Hull special units. Professor Keith Bottomley, Professor Norman Jepson, Mr Kenneth Elliott and Dr Jeremy Coid. 1994. (Available from the RSD Information and Publications Group).

The Nacro diversion initiative for mentally disturbed offenders: an account and an evaluation. Home Office, NACRO and Mental Health Foundation. 1994. (Available from the RSD Information and Publications Group).

Probation Motor Projects in England and Wales. J P Martin and Douglas Martin. 1994.

Community-based treatment of sex offenders: an evaluation of seven treatment programmes. R Beckett, A Beech, D Fisher and A S Fordham. 1994.

Videotaping children's evidence: an evaluation. Graham Davies, Clare Wilson, Rebecca Mitchell and John Milsom. 1995.

Managing the needs of female prisoners. Allison Morris, Chris Wilkinson, Andrea Tisi, Jane Woodrow and Ann Rockley. 1995.

Local information points for volunteers. Michael Locke, Nick Richards, Lorraine Down, Jon Griffiths and Roger Worgan. 1995.

Mental disorder in remand prisoners. Anthony Maden, Caecilia J. A. Taylor, Deborah Brooke and John Gunn. 1996.

An evaluation of prison work and training. Frances Simon and Claire Corbett. 1996.

The Impact of the National Lottery on the Horse-Race Betting Levy. Simon Field. 1996.

Books

Analysing Offending. Data, Models and Interpretations. Roger Tarling. 1993. viii + 203pp. (0 11 341080 8).

Requests for Publications

Home Office Research Studies from 143 onwards, *Research and Planning Unit Papers, Research Findings and Research Bulletins* are available **subject to availability** on request from:

Research and Statistics Directorate
Information and Publications Group
Room 1308, Home Office
Apollo House
36 Wellesley Road
Croydon CR9 3RR
Telephone: 0181 760 8340
Fascimile: 0181 760 8364
Internet: http/www.open.gov.u/home_off/rsdhome.htm
E-mail: rsd.ha apollo @ gtnet.gov.u.

Occasional Papers can be purchased from:
Home Office
Publications Unit
50 Queen Anne's Gate
London SW1H 9AT
Telephone: 0171 273 2302

Home Office Research Studies prior to 143 can be purchased from:

HMSO Publications Centre

(Mail, fax and telephone orders only)
PO Box 276, London SW8 5DT
Telephone orders: 0171-873 9090
General enquiries: 0171-873 0011
(queuing system in operation for both numbers)
Fax orders: 0171-873 8200

*And also from **HMSO Bookshops***